NATURE AND RENEWAL

NATURE AND RENEWAL

Wild River Valley and Beyond

Dean B. Bennett

Original Pen-and-Ink Drawings by the Author

TILBURY HOUSE PUBLISHERS
GARDINER, MAINE

Tilbury House, Publishers
103 Brunswick Avenue
Gardiner, Maine 04345
800–582–1899 • www.tilburyhouse.com

First paperback edition: October 2009
10 9 8 7 6 5 4 3 2 1

Text and illustrations copyright © 2009 by Dean B. Bennett

Library of Congress Cataloging-in-Publication Data
Bennett, Dean B.
  Nature and renewal : Wild River Valley and beyond / Dean B. Bennett ; original pen-and-ink drawings by the author. -- 1st pbk. ed.
    p. cm.
  Includes bibliographical references and index.
  ISBN 978-0-88448-325-0 (pbk. : alk. paper)
  1. Wilderness areas--Wild River Valley (N.H. and Me.) 2. Natural history--Wild River Valley (N.H. and Me.) 3. Logging--Environmental aspects--Wild River Valley (N.H. and Me.) 4. Wild River Valley (N.H. and Me.)--History I. Title.
  QH76.5.W55B46 2009
  508.741--dc22

                              2009030536

Cover photograph by Dean B. Bennett
Cover designed by Geraldine Millham, Westport, Massachusetts
Copyedited by Genie Dailey, Fine Points Editorial Services, Jefferson, Maine
Printed and bound by Versa Press, East Peoria, Illinois

To Sheila

CONTENTS

Preface

It was totally unexpected. A forester inventorying stands of trees was deep in an isolated, well-forested valley at the foot of a mountain when he saw a hemlock tree of great girth, far exceeding any trees nearby. "The diameter caught my attention," he said later. "I wouldn't be surprised if it were 300 years old."[1]

Anyone who sees the tree and knows what had occurred in this valley would be astonished. Those who come into the valley today drive over what was once a railroad that brought loggers from its thriving community deep into its virgin forests. Over the years the steep hillsides were clear-cut, made barren and naked, ready for the floods and fires that would come and destroy much of the rest. The once vibrant village of Hastings—with residences, boardinghouses, mills, barns and sheds, a store, post office, and even a school—is now gone! In 1999, when the forester made his surprising discovery of the big tree, the once deforested valley contained a mature forest reclaimed by nature where, against all odds, there still stood a remnant of the wilderness that had come before. What's more, less than a decade later, the old tree would receive a guarantee that it could live out the rest of its life in a place that would only become wilder. Today, the valley contains a wilderness embedded with artifacts of a rich human history, making it, indeed, a living museum.

Thanks to America's Wilderness Act of 1964 and the vision and dedication of many citizens, thousands of acres in the valley, known as Wild River Valley, which lies in the White Mountain National Forest, are now protected within the National Wilderness Preservation System. The valley is now a prime example of the idea that areas once severely damaged by destructive land-use practices can become candidates for wilderness preservation, where nature is allowed to reclaim them, and where visitors can find solitude, peace, and quiet. Its preservation provides revealing parallels with such work going on all across the nation as described in the Afterword.

How many who are venturing into these wilderness areas today are aware that their gear or outdoor wear may have evolved from the experience of a thirteen-year-old on his first hunting trip into Wild River Valley? Leon Leonwood Bean's many trips into the valley were among those that spawned his interest in developing comfortable outdoor footwear prior to his establishment of the world-famous firm, L. L. Bean. It was 1911 when Bean invented his famous shoe. That same year clear-cutting in the valley and throughout the White Mountains prompted Congress to pass the Weeks Act protecting lands in the watersheds of navigable streams. Less than three weeks after the act was signed by President Howard Taft, the chief of the Forest Service singled out Wild River Valley for purchase.

There are other reasons why the story of Wild River Valley is so compelling. One hundred miles southeast of Wild River, in a comparable valley of the White Mountain National Forest, a long-running and widely recognized investigation in the Hubbard Brook Experimental Forest helps explain the effects of the classic case of clear-cutting in Wild River Valley. Today, data from decades of studies at Hubbard Brook are also of interest in detecting environmental change due to global warming, something unimagined in the heyday of the former logging community of Hastings. The old village's history captures attention for several reasons: the community contained perhaps the only wood alcohol mill in Maine, and in the mid-1890s, it had electric lighting little more than a decade after the first city in the United States had electric lights. In its essence, however, the story of Wild River Valley is one of dreams fulfilled and unfulfilled, of tragedy and good fortune, of land abuse and stewardship, of nature's vulnerability and resiliency, of seeing into the future from the past. There is a message for everyone.

ACKNOWLEDGMENTS

As a reader, I always find the acknowledgments section of a book interesting because it gives me clues to how the author worked—how broadly and deeply he or she looked for information on which the book is based. I gain some feeling about the book's authenticity and the diversity of ideas and subjects it covers. For example, this book is about a place, but when you scan the acknowledgments below, you will begin to see that it connects to places all across the continent, from Maine to Alaska and from Minnesota to Mississippi, and relates to changes in our culture's views toward nature that span a time from the distant past to the present.

From the author's perspective, however, the acknowledgments section is an opportunity to publicly express a thank-you to each of those who helped bring an idea into the form of a book. In the case of this book, there were many individuals who contributed their time, energy, and thoughts over the several years of research and writing that it took to bring it to completion.

First, I thank my wife, Sheila, who has been a guiding force behind all my books. Her steady support, clear advice, and companionship throughout this project have been crucial to its development. She has been a sounding board for ideas as I crafted the book, a reader and helpful critic of its many drafts, and a fellow explorer on numerous hiking trips into Wild River Valley.

I thank the following individuals who read and commented on various chapters of the book: Jerry Bley, Douglas Schwarz, and Daniel Yetter. Their comments were especially helpful in writing chapters 6, 7, and 8.

I also thank the many individuals, private organizations, and public agencies and institutions for their interest, support, and information. Among them, I am especially indebted to the following:

For field trips and hikes into the valley to learn about its natural and human history, I thank Lyle Wiggin, retiree of the Forest Service, White Mountain National Forest, and Arthur "Joe" Taylor, also of the Forest Service, White Mountain National Forest. I benefited immensely from their knowledge of the valley's natural environment and the history and remnants of the old village of Hastings, logging camps, and Wild River Railroad. Lyle also helped me in finding many documents relating to the history of the valley and Hastings, and unselfishly shared many of his personal papers throughout my research. Joe guided me on four trips into the valley, covering many miles of trails and features, including a newly discovered, amazingly intact section of the old railroad. Joe has a long history with the valley. He is the son of Harry Taylor, Sr., who grew up in Hastings Village in one of a row of houses called the "Ten Commandments" situated along the bank of Wild River and who later became a well-known logger in the region. I thank, too, Heather Dowey and Ryan Owens of The Wilderness Society who were companions on a pleasant hike one day on the Wild River Trail. Heather also was a constant source of information during my research on the issues and process of preserving the valley as wilderness.

I thank Stanley Howe and Randall Bennett of the Bethel [Maine] Historical Society for many important sources of information on the valley's history, and also Barbara Hastings Honkala, who works with them and who contributed valuable information about the Hastings family. I appreciate the help I received from Earle G. Shettleworth, Jr., of the Maine Historic Preservation Commission, in obtaining photographs. I also thank Howard Reiche and Hugh Chapman of the Gilead [Maine] Historical Society for their insights into Hastings and the valley's logging history. Nancy E. Petrie's efforts to locate information in the *Northern Logger and Timber Processer* magazine were much appreciated. I am grateful to Bill Gove for generously sharing information, and especially his map of the Wild River Railroad. I thank David C. Smith for his leads to sources of information about the alcohol mill at Hastings, and Richard A. Hale for helpful information related to the operation of such mills. Both are emeritus professors at the University of Maine. I'm grateful to Stephanie Philbrick for her efforts to locate information at the Maine Historical Society, to Suzann Coburn and Jeanne Daigle for their help at the Gorham [New Hampshire] Public Library, and to the staff at the Maine State Library for their pleasant and helpful assistance. I thank Clifford F. Biron of the Island Pond [Vermont] Historical Society, Inc., for his help in researching Samuel D. Hobson and Vermont connections to Wild River Lumber Company and its operation.

I especially thank Walter W. Wintturi for his information about the old hemlock and for the directions to its location. This tree became a key element in the story of the valley. I'm also grateful to others who helped me with information about the natural environment of the valley and the protection of its ecosystems. Among them are Gabriella Howard, Bennett Katz Library, University of Maine at Augusta; John Campbell, United States Forest Service, Northeastern Research Station; Steven Hamburg, Brown University; Heidi Overbeck, Environment Maine; Robert G. Marvinney and Woodrow B. Thompson, Bureau of Geology and Natural Areas, Maine Department of Conservation; and Sara Cairns and Brett Engstrom, New Hampshire Natural History Inventory.

I am also grateful for the assistance I received from the United States Forest Service, and I especially thank the following of the White Mountain National Forest: Tom Wagner, Joe Gill, Fred Kacprzynski, Wayne Millen, David Neely, Chris O'Brien, Rebecca Oreskes, Karl Roenke, Matt Schomburg, Arthur "Joe" Taylor, and Susan Cone. I also thank David Lacy of the Green Mountain National Forest.

I thank a number of individuals who helped me with information about wilderness preservation and efforts to protect Wild River Valley, especially the following: Heather Dowey, Bart Koehler, Melyssa Watson, and Julie Wormser—all of The Wilderness Society—and Jerry Bley of Creative Conservation. A special thank-you must be given to the Friends of Wild River and to the following who were especially helpful in my understanding of their long and persevering effort to preserve the New Hampshire side of the valley as wilderness: Dan Yetter, Tom Merrick, Tom Van Vechten, Ross Newcomb, Dick Palmer, Doug Schwarz, and George Haselton.

Wilderness preservationists across the United States helped me put the Wild River Valley story into a larger context and give it a broader perspective. I especially thank the following: Douglas W. Scott, the Campaign for America's Wilderness; Kirk Johnson, Friends of Allegheny Wilderness; Jim Murray, Virginia Wilderness Committee; David Saville, Helen McGinnis, and Matt Keller—all of the West Virginia Wilderness Coalition; Davis Mounger, Friends of Mississippi Public Lands; Brent Martin, Georgia Forest Watch; Sarah Strommen, Friends of the Boundary Waters Wilderness; Jan Swensen, Badlands Conservation Alliance; Heather Morijah, Sierra Club, South Dakota West River Office; Rich Csenge, Mainers for Utah Wilderness; Don Hoffman, Katurah Mackay, Matt Skroach, Jason Williams, and Kim Crumbo—all of the Arizona Wilderness Coalition; Shaaron Netherton and Jeremy Garncarz, Friends of Nevada Wilderness; Regina Merritt, Oregon Wild Campaign; Bill Marlett, Oregon Natural Desert Association; Chris Soderstrom, Alaska Rainforest Campaign; Katya Kirsh, Southeast Alaska Conservation Council; and Duane Short, Illinois forest activist.

Finally, I thank Jennifer Bunting, publisher of Tilbury House, for bringing the story of Wild River Valley and its message to the public and for her enthusiastic support.

Dean B. Bennett
Mt. Vernon, Maine

PART I

BEFORE THE FIRE

One

Magnificent Wildness

It stands meditatively in deep silence, partly because everything is still, not a branch or an animal moves. The rippling stream below is already muffled by the early snowstorm. Overhead, a phosphorescent moon fills the valley with soft white light, and the great tree casts its shadow on the mountainside, sharply etched on the new-fallen snow. The cold plunges deeper, knifing into the old hemlock's bark, but it's nothing new: the tree has withstood harsh winters in this country for centuries. Then a sharp clap rings out, like a rifle being fired, echoing from mountain to mountain in the clear air. Somewhere nearby, the chill has been too much for a tree, and it cracked open with an explosive snap, a familiar sound to loggers, but they are now gone from the valley and with them an entire village of homes and mills and the railroad. The woodland surrounding the tree returns to a quiet peacefulness.

The tree is alone, if judged by its age, in the middle of a valley named after the river, Wild River. The river, in turn, got its name from its sudden shift in character from a gentle coursing stream to a frothy, rampaging torrent of white water during spring runoff and sudden rainstorms. Surrounded by high mountains, the river begins quietly in the marshy, mountain-ringed basin of No Ketchum Pond and flows down the valley with increasing enthusiasm and noise, dodging more and more rocks, passing the old hemlock five and a half miles down, and in another five and a half miles sweeping by the old ghost town of Hastings where it meets up with its major tributary, Evans Brook, beneath the ledges of the popular overlook, The Roost. Reinvigorated by an injection of swift-flowing mountain water from the Evans Brook and Evans Notch arm of the valley, the river would seem poised for its final rollicking three-mile dash to join the Androscoggin River, one of Maine's largest. But the river quickly loses its punch to topography, for it flattens out and makes a

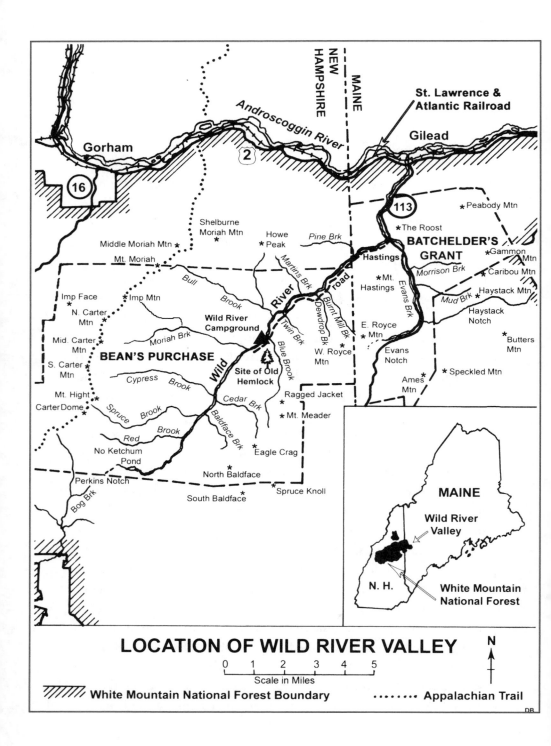

LOCATION OF WILD RIVER VALLEY

Scale in Miles: 0 1 2 3 4 5

N

////// White Mountain National Forest Boundary ········· Appalachian Trail

rather quiet entry into the Androscoggin after passing beneath Route 2 and the St. Lawrence & Atlantic Railroad in the village of Gilead, Maine.

The old hemlock and the river are conjoined by an effusion of water confined in the valley it made, filtering downward through seepages and springs, rivulets, brooks, and streams. For centuries, perhaps half the hemlock's life, the two existed in a valley of peace, tranquility, grandeur, and magnificent wildness, remote from the world outside. Even today, the valley's headwaters around No Ketchum Pond lie in remote country: it takes a long hike through deep mountain forests to reach the pond from any direction. An aura of mystery still emanates from this place, giving the valley a wild quality and mystique found in so many wilderness areas. But within the last two hundred years, the mystery diminished as the hemlock and river witnessed devastating changes to the ordered world in which they lived, changes that inflicted ecological damage that still to this day is being repaired by a slow process of natural healing.

The old hemlock and the river share the effects of a nearly incomprehensible natural history that has been traced with degrees of accuracy to hundreds of millions of years ago.[1] The story of the very underpinning of the hemlock and river, the foundation bedrock on which they rest, is one of ancient seas filled layer by layer with sediment washed off surrounding mountains until they were gone, of compaction and rock formation, of drifting continents and their collisions, of mountain building and more rock formation—all, quite unbelievably, happening near the equator before the continent moved to higher latitudes where snow swirls around the roots of trees and their bark cracks open when they freeze.

Still, nature was not through roughing out the valley's form. It needed to rasp, grind, and smooth here and fill in there. It was slow work, beginning 25,000 or so years ago, when a monstrous sheet of ice, ominously grinding, creaking, and inching its way from the northwest, crossed at right angles to the length of the valley.[2] The glacier's enormous weight pulverized the rocks beneath it and embedded them in its bottom layers of ice, in effect turning the massive ice sheet into a great abrasive tool. It ground its way up over the northwest flanks of the

The valley of Wild River from The Roost. The Roost is a popular overlook on open ledges above the confluence of Evans Brook and Wild River at the northeast corner of the valley. PHOTOGRAPH BY DEAN B. BENNETT

Evans Notch and the valley of Evans Brook from The Roost
PHOTOGRAPH BY DEAN B. BENNETT

Wild River—quiet waters in the lower part
Photograph by Dean B. Bennett

valley's surrounding mountains, smoothing, scratching, and grooving the ancient bedrock and molding the slopes into ramp-like shapes. As it reached the tops of the mountains and ridges, it slumped down, prying and breaking off rocks and leaving ledges and cliffs on the southeast sides.

A few thousand years later, the climate warmed and the glacier began to melt, thin out, and retreat northward. By 13,000 years ago, it had left the valley. Mountain streams rushed down barren slopes strewn with boulders and rocks that had dropped out of the ice as it melted. The streams carried loads of sand and gravel down into the valley, grinding and shaping the bedrock before dumping their loads into lowland basins and streambeds.

From the time the glacier left, the valley's streams have continued

Wild River—spring runoff in rocky rapids
PHOTOGRAPH BY DEAN B. BENNETT

the work of wearing down the bedrock and carrying away sediments, building sand and gravel terraces, and developing small flood plains at their mouths, which, in turn, are being dissected by the same streams that built them. One particular flood plain lies between Evans Brook and Wild River near their junction. What happened here would change the valley more than anything it had ever experienced.

Revegetation of the valley's barren landscape began immediately following the retreat of the glacier. Lichens, mosses, sedges, and grasses appeared, but it took several hundred years before the plants provided sufficient cover to prevent rivulets, brooks, and streams from severely eroding the landscape. Gradually soil accumulated as the plants took root and captured nutrients from the weathering bedrock and glacial debris and added their own organic matter. A succession of plant life followed as soil conditions became more favorable to higher and higher orders of plants. Eventually trees found enough soil to take root. Forests in the valley were heavily canopied by trees of many ages, including giant, ancient trees. These were trees, such as hemlocks, that could survive in dense shade, growing slowly until they were given an opening to grow into large, mature trees. Such openings in the forested landscape were created by insect damage, forest fires, and wind-downed trees.

The lineage of the valley's old hemlock, if traced back in time, would reveal that its ancestors entered the valley between 8,000 and 5,000 years ago.[3] That was a time, following the disappearance of the glacier, when the climate began to warm. The change in temperature drew the hemlock's forebears in great numbers from warmer southern areas into what is today called Maine and New Hampshire. The species was not alone in its march northward; beech and yellow birch accompanied it.

The hemlock species had hardly established a solid foothold when disaster struck. Five thousand years ago, according to the story revealed by pollen in soil samples, a massive die-off began, almost in synchrony across its entire range and probably the result of a virulent pathogen. Wild River Valley lost most, if not all, of its hemlock population. The disappearance has been likened to the fate suffered by the American chestnut in the early twentieth century. The hemlock, however, would not give up. After a few hundred years, hemlock pollen grains once again began to appear in northern New England's soil samples. The hemlock population slowly recovered, perhaps because not all trees were vulnerable to the supposed pathogen.

Sometime around 1,500 to 1,000 years ago, the hemlock population once again began to decrease as spruce and fir of the boreal forest slowly expanded their ranges southward, this time perhaps due to climatic cooling in north temperate latitudes. The hemlock species lost some of its status in the forest, but it did not disappear. Instead, it became a common rather than a dominant member of most forest communities. Such was the case with hemlocks in certain plant communities in Wild River Valley.

Science has provided us with clues to the history of hemlock populations, but what about an individual, such as the old hemlock in Wild

River Valley, that survived against almost impossible odds in its natural world but then faced a world thrust on it by a species that brought destruction to the delicate ecological balance in which it had successfully survived? What about its origin, its life, and the world in which it lived? If it could only speak, we wish. Fortunately, we know enough to imagine with some basis in scientific fact what life was like for that old tree.

* * *

The story of the old hemlock could have begun in the early 1600s, just before the time Europeans began to settle New England's coastal lands. The hemlock's parent tree may have stood on a gentle, south-facing slope, as do the majority of trees of this species.[4] On a spring day it would have been shedding pollen from its tiny flowers.[5] Perhaps a light breeze blew, scattering the tiny grains over a wide area, some drifting down the valley. We know that a pollen grain responsible for the old hemlock came to rest on a sticky surface between two scales of a small cone attached to the branch of another hemlock. The tree was less than a thousand feet from a brook, now named Blue Brook, a tributary of the river. The brook would have been running full and vigorous from the melting snow that undoubtedly still whitened the tops of the surrounding mountains. This was a remarkable event in the life of the pollen grain when all but a few of the untold numbers being shed were destined to be carried away by the river or to find a resting spot on the ground, never to fulfill their purpose. On the upper surface of each scale between which the pollen grain resided, were two structures called ovules, each containing an egg. Over the course of the next few months, while the river ebbed and flowed, a small tube grew from the pollen grain to one of the eggs, and through it sperm made their way from the pollen to fertilize the egg. A tiny seed began to form, containing an embryo tree with leaves, stem, and root point. About half of the seed was winged.

That fall the cone matured, and during the winter, the seed fell onto the snowpack covering the ground. When the warming temperature of

Old forest in the White Mountains
UNITED STATES FOREST SERVICE, WHITE MOUNTAIN NATIONAL FOREST PHOTOGRAPH

spring began melting the snow, the seed settled down onto the moist, shaded forest floor beneath the parent hemlock. The growing embryo split its shell, and a root point emerged, penetrating the cool, damp soil to absorb water and food. By the end of the summer, a tiny seedling emerged. It is probable that the young tree grew slowly in a deeply shaded area of the forest. And we know that it escaped fatal injury from serious threats such as those posed by browsing snowshoe hares and gnawing mice and squirrels.

The hemlock's neighboring forest trees likely would have included other hemlocks, a few red spruce and balsam fir, some white pine, and numerous hardwood species, including sugar maple, beech, yellow and white birch, and aspen—characteristic of the lower slopes and mountain valleys. Above the hemlock on the higher slopes where shallower soils overlaid bedrock, red spruce, fir, and some birch dominated. Below the hemlock in the lower parts of the valley were beech and other hardwoods, white pine, hemlock, and, in a few places, red spruce.[6]

In such an undisturbed old forest, a few scattered trees would have grown to immense size while others in the understory would have been smaller, surviving on only the small amount of light that filtered through the dense canopy. Strewn over the forest floor were the remains of windblown trees in all stages of decay, some only mossy mounds. On the high mountainsides and rocky mountain summits, the vegetation consisted of mosses, lichens, heath plants, and stunted spruce and birch. They were suited to harsher conditions and hinted of earlier times in the years following recession of the glacier.

In the sheltered valley of Wild River, few storms have been recorded that reached a velocity that could destroy its forests. This is fortunate for the eastern hemlock species because we have observed that the tree's full crown and shallow root system make it susceptible to windthrow.[7] However, from historic hurricane data, we know that a severe storm swept through the vicinity of Wild River Valley in 1788.[8] Whether the storm downed the hemlock's parent tree or it succumbed to old age or some other cause, we don't know, but its eventual removal is a certainty. When it did happen, it is quite likely that an opening was left which would have allowed the hemlock sapling, perhaps for the first time in its life, to receive the full, direct rays of the sun. The light would have had a profound effect on the young hemlock, stimulating it to grow at a phenomenal rate compared to its first shade-bound years.

As the hemlock grew, it increasingly contributed to a natural community that drew on millions of years of evolution involving an incalculable number of random steps, each tested one against the other, some discarded, others successful, some short-lived, others lasting, but all responsible for the beauty, diversity, and dynamic stability of the forests in the valley. The hemlock's life was connected in countless ways, many still unknown, with other living and nonliving things that made up the ecological complexity of the valley. As it grew larger, the tree would have attracted a diversity of animals, for example, sapsuckers that have a liking for the juicy cambium layer beneath the bark of hemlock trees and proceed to ring them with feeding holes.

By the year 1800 the hemlock was probably well established in its forest community and may have drawn a variety of nesting birds adapted to the valley's ecosystems. Broad-winged hawks are known to nest in hemlock trees, constructing sheltered, well-built nests of sticks and twigs twenty to forty feet above the ground. This species of hawk is rather small and chunky with black bands on its tail and rounded, black-tipped wings. Other hawks also may have nested in the tree. The sharp-shinned hawk, smaller than the broad-winged, is a woodland hawk named for its thin tarsus, or shank, that part of the foot just above the toes. Secretive and preferring undisturbed forests, this hawk would be at home in the hemlock's community. It, like the broad-winged hawk, has its nest of sticks anchored to a limb near the trunk of a tree. Another hawk is the northern goshawk, who is known to strip bark from hemlock trees to line its nest.

The hemlock also could have provided a home for other birds, such as black-throated green warblers, who are known to build their cup-shaped nests in hemlock trees, perhaps as high as twenty feet above the ground. The small, yellow-faced birds with olive-green crowns and black throats would have added a bit of color to the tree. The warblers' territory is customarily limited to about two acres, and in that space, the birds are in constant motion, flitting here and there, hovering, and pecking in amongst the leaves of trees and shrubs looking for insects.

The hemlock likely contributed the larvae of several insects to the food supply that warblers and other small birds desired. One might have been the bicolored moth, gray in color with pale yellow body parts—an insect that lays eggs from which caterpillars emerge that eat hemlock needles. The same is true for a number of other moths: the lightly patterned, grayish-brown, pale-marked angle; the brownish-gray hemlock angle; and the whitish, brown-speckled porcelain gray.

The black-throated warblers may have found resident spiders useful. Spiders provide silk from their webs that black-throated green warblers use in the construction of their nests to augment more substantial materials such as lichens, mosses, grasses, and twigs. And of course, the spiders themselves become food for the warblers. Among the spiders that could have lived in the hemlock is the eight-eyed *Uloborus americanus* that makes a horizontal orb web. When an insect is caught, the spider throws silk over it and wraps it firmly. Another spider is the oval-shaped triangle spider, *Hyptiotes cavatus*. Its common name comes from the shape of its web, which consists of four strands of silk spun from a common point and expanding outward to form a triangle. The spider weaves many threads across the four threads, and then it waits at the apex of the triangle, ready to grab any prey animal that is caught and take it back to its perch for eating.

The tree may have attracted a number of transient visitors. Porcupines are known to spend time around hemlock trees, nibbling their branches and leaving piles of twigs scattered beneath them. Other visitors could have included ruffed grouse feeding on buds and leaves, and black-capped chickadees, red crossbills, and pine siskins feeding on the hemlock's prodigious quantities of small, winged seeds. And perhaps when it was younger and its branches swept low to the ground, grouse and deer had used it from time to time for winter cover. Even a silver-haired bat may have roosted in it.

In its undisturbed setting, the hemlock's influence also extended in other ways to its surroundings. Its monolayered branches and needles not only created a shade-saturated understory beneath the tree, they broke the fall of raindrops from heavy mountain showers and distributed the water, making the hillside a little less vulnerable to the effects of erosion. The tree's shallow and extensive root system also tended to stabilize the soil, keeping it in place.

Beneath the tree its fallen, decaying needle-leaves added nitrogen to the soil. The needles also contained tannin, an acidic compound, which increased the acidity of the soil. The same chemical resided in the hemlock's bark, and at a time in the distant future, hemlocks in the valley would entice bark cutters in search of hemlocks to harvest for the tanning industry.

The soil into which the hemlock extended its broadening root system had taken thousands of years to develop and was still continuing its slow buildup at the rate of hundreds of years per inch of depth. The hemlock's roots took in nutrients from the soil that the tree needed to live and grow. But the hemlock would not have been alone in this process, for on the forest floor beneath the tree's overhanging branches there grew mushrooms. One could have been the species *Tricholoma viscidipes*. It has a slimy stem, a cap that is dry and whitish, and a pungent odor to the nose of anything that might sniff it. Hemlocks have a special association with the mushroom, for the fungus is able to help them obtain necessary nutrients from the soil. It is a symbiotic relationship, known today as a micorrhizal association. The fungus has microscopic tubular, threadlike filaments, called hyphae, that secrete enzymes necessary for the breakdown of decaying matter and absorption of nutrients and energy. The hyphae penetrate roots of trees, allowing nutrients to move through the fungus into the trees' cells. The fungus, in return, receives needed organic compounds that are produced in the tree's needles through photosynthesis. The fungus's hyphae develop into a large, complex network called a mycelium, which increases the ability of the fungus to provide nutrients to trees. Each mushroom growing beneath trees is actually a mass of sexually reproductive, mycelium-producing spores.

Birds that may have lived in the hemlock would have extended the tree's connection with its community and valley. A broad-winged hawk's territory stretches to a mile or more as it searches for prey. It hunts along the edges of streams, and ponds, along the river, and in marshy areas looking for frogs, snakes, small birds, and crayfish. In the forest, the hawk looks for red squirrels, chipmunks, mice, and shrews. The sharp-shinned hawk hunts a wider area, flying just above the trees or whipping through openings in the woods in search of small birds, although it could take larger birds, such as a pileated woodpecker.

Gliding over the tops and high slopes of the surrounding mountains, the hawks would have been able to see the entire valley and the hunting grounds it contained. During these early years in the hemlock's life, the valley's vegetation would have been undisturbed. Shadows would have broken the dense forest where the river flowed, revealing a dark, irregular line snaking up the valley, bisecting it at its greatest depth. Similarly, the routes of the river's tributaries would have been discernible, marking side basins and ravines. All of the valley's waterways would have offered the hawks secluded avenues through the forest to favorite hunting areas.

Birds of prey would have been attracted to the headwaters of the river and the small pond ringed by a band of marshland and a dense forest of spruce and fir. Here they could have sat on perches and waited patiently for the appearance of amphibians, small mammals, and birds. Some of these birds would also have been attracted to the open areas of the ledges of mountaintops and ridges surrounding the valley. Only a mile to the southeast of the hemlock, the land rises to exposed granitic outcrops high above the tree. Here, after the glacier had left, lichens in concert with the weather had begun the process of soil building. In fact, the hardy lichens had been the first to appear. Being both a fungus that provides structure and anchoring and a photosynthesizing alga that produces food, a lichen is uniquely able to survive where no soil exists. Patches of the rusty red, gray-orange disk lichen and the greenish-gray concentric boulder lichen would have likely decorated the rocks. These crustose lichens are early pioneers on ledges, where they speed up the weathering process and make rock surfaces a little more soluble for other kinds of lichens, such as the leafy folios Cumberland rock-shield lichen and the late-appearing, shrubby fruticose lichens—red-capped British soldiers and silver-gray reindeer lichen.

The remains of previous generations of lichens and the dust particles trapped by them had added to the patches of soil, providing places for juniper hair-cap moss, mountain witchgrass, and northern bentgrass to take root and grow. Other plant life undoubtedly included the low-tufted fern rusty woodsia, shrub meadowsweet that displays pinkish-white conical clusters of tiny flowers in season, low blueberry, and a scattering of weather-wracked trees such as heart-leaved white birch, red spruce, and balsam fir. This succession of plant life was followed by insects, including tiger beetles, bee flies, butterflies and moths such as the brown elfin butterfly and the white-marked tussock moth, and spiders, for example, the barn spider. This community, in turn, attracted other residents and visitors such as dark-eyed juncos and garter snakes.

The hemlock and the other life in the valley, then as today, was dependent on the valley's river, mountain streams, small ponds, varied bogs, and complex network of rivulets and underground seeps, for they formed an intricate meshwork of pathways for the flow of water—a fancy embroidered pattern of moving water funneling downward to the mouth of the river, interconnecting the living and nonliving components of the valley's ecosystems. As the water flowed through the valley, it made a relatively constant supply of nutrients, such as nitrogen, phosphorous, and sulfur, available to the valley's living things. All were enmeshed in cycles that involved the valley's water, air, and rocks in supplying essential nutrient matter to a pyramid-like arrangement of organisms consisting of large numbers of plant producers at the base upon which depended fewer animal herbivores and even fewer carnivores.

Up to the early 1800s, the valley's ecological condition was little disturbed by humans. The ecosystems exhibited an advanced state of development characterized by a large number of different living things occupying much of its space, many of which specialized in its resources, grew more slowly, reached larger sizes, and had longer life cycles. These conditions were made possible because, through the years, the valley had experienced relatively few serious natural disturbances, such as severe forest fires and devastating hurricanes or other storms, which could have interrupted succession and produced stress on ecosystems. Its climate, seasonal variation, and high quality of water and air had been relatively unchanging and dependable. Thus, the valley had reached a state where changes continued to occur, but more slowly, and where there existed a greater resistance to disturbance.

This, then, is the story of the hemlock's life in the forested wilderness of Wild River Valley before the fateful change it was to witness. It had taken thousands of years for the valley to reach the state of development it possessed by the beginning of the nineteenth century. All that, however, would be uprooted, for there was another presence that from time to time had roamed the surrounding region well before the hemlock began its life. It was a species that would one day disturb the natural world of the hemlock and its valley in ways that would change it forever.

Two

HUMAN PRESENCE

The first humans to enter the valley probably did so before the old hemlock began its life. Scientists have determined that people arrived in the valley's region between 10,000 and 11,000 years ago, perhaps two thousand years after the glacier left. They were given the name Paleoindian, meaning old, or ancient, native peoples.[1]

During the first thousand years following the glacier's retreat, the valley and the surrounding lands still contained treeless tundra growth on the tops of tall mountains.[2] The tundra communities consisted of lichens, mosses, sedges, grasses, and dwarf trees and shrubs. But the land the Paleoindians encountered in the valleys was well underway to becoming a closed woodland forest in response to a warming climate, and already in many areas, it was changing from a mixed woodland dominated by spruce, birch, aspen, and alder to white pine, birch, and oak. These native people came into this environment for the same reason others would be attracted to the area throughout millennia up to the present, a reason that would ultimately cause a severe interruption to the valley's long, natural evolution: they came in pursuit of its natural resources.

These people are still shrouded in myster due to our poor knowledge of them and their culture. We know that they were hunters and gatherers, and although we are limited to what we can infer from the tools and fragments of worked stone they left at various locations, we are given clues to their skills at designing and manufacturing implements, their means of subsistence, their routes of travel, the length of time they were present in the region, and their relationships to other cultures across North America.

We surmise that they were attracted to hunting grounds frequented by large mammals, most likely caribou and possibly other large animals such as the woolly mammoth and musk ox. And we know that they sought desirable stone for their tools and weapons. This is evidenced at Mount Jasper, which overlooks the Androscoggin River sixteen miles to the north of the valley near Berlin, New Hampshire. The mountain yields rhyolite, a dense, hard rock of microscopic crystals. It occurs in dikes—long, narrow masses of igneous rock (rock that was once molten) that was forced into fissures of the volcanic rock from which the mountain was formed hundreds of millions of years ago.

About sixty-five feet below the summit, the natives quarried nearly thirty feet into the mountain, following a dike from which they mined the rhyolite. They set up work stations at the summit and at the foot of the mountain for their tool-making operations. Rhyolite was especially sought out because of its hardness and workability. When struck at the correct angle by a hard object, it flakes off, producing conchoidal depressions—shallow grooves called flutes. Both faces of a rock were often expertly worked by striking sharp blows or applying pressure using hard objects until a desired shape was obtained. In this way the natives produced projectile points, skinning and butchering tools, scrapers, knives, and other implements.

It is likely that these early people entered the valley of Wild River in their search for game animals, edible plants, and quality stone for tools and weapons. The nearness of Mount Jasper, the discovery of a flensing, or butchering, tool only fourteen and one-half miles to the west of the valley in Randolph, and the fact that artifact locations suggest travel along corridors associated with streams and rivers all support this possibility.

As trees spread over the region around 10,000 years ago, so did wildlife species experience a shift.[3] From that time on, wildlife populations fluctuated with forest conditions, which, in turn, responded to a changing climate.[4] For example, about 8,000 to 5,000 years ago, hemlock began to intrude into the existing forest of white pine, birch, and oak, followed by beech and yellow birch. Where hemlock densely dominated the forests, the forest floor and understory was shaded and moist with a minimum of trees and shrubs. In such a situation, deer would find less favorable forage and would be less numerous. Then around 5,000 years ago, the hemlock component of the forest declined precipitously, later recovering and thriving up to about 1,000 years ago. Conditions changed yet again, and by the time colonists and settlers had invaded the region and begun cutting hemlock for its bark, the species was already in another decline.

The changes in environment during post-glacial time influenced the cultures of indigenous peoples inhabiting the region.[5] With the growth of large trees sometime early in a time period archaeologists call the Archaic, about 10,000 to 3,000 years ago, the dugout canoe came into being. Patterns of travel reflected more than ever the systems of rivers, streams, and lakes. Territories were influenced by boundaries of watersheds. Then, in a time period called the Ceramic, roughly from 3,000 years ago to European contact around 500 years ago, several innovations contributed to cultural change among indigenous populations. These included the making of pottery and the development of the birchbark canoe, both of which occurred early in the period. Another cultural shift came with agriculture and the growing of beans, corn, and squash.

Throughout these periods of indigenous history, artifacts show continuous mining of rhyolite at Mount Jasper for the production of tools and implements. The presence of native people, called Amarascoggin or Androscoggin,[6] near Wild River Valley was established by the discovery of a post-European–contact, Native settlement located on rich, intervale land along the banks of the Androscoggin River about eight miles south of the mouth of Wild River near Bethel, Maine. It is conjectured that the village existed well into the 1700s.[7] This Native village was connected to another Native village, that of the Pigwackets, in the Saco River basin at what is now Fryeburg, Maine. Natives could travel to that village by way of the Androscoggin River and a primitive trail that followed Wild River at Gilead up to the river's confluence with Evans Brook, along the brook through Evans Notch, and down the Cold River to the Saco River, a distance of perhaps twenty miles.

The people who lived in the region of Wild River Valley just prior to the first major wave of European immigrants were known as Eastern Abenaki, from their own name *Wapanahki* (often referred to as Wabanaki in a broad sense), or dawn land people.[8] The lifestyles of these indigenous people were closely related to the seasonal availability of food. We believe that these natives of the upper Androscoggin only resided in their villages for a few months out of a year, spending the rest of the time in camps of small family bands.[9] In the summer, they moved their encampments to the coast for fishing and hunting and in the fall and winter, inland for hunting and trapping. Harvesting occurred in the fall. For example, the site of the old village on the Androscoggin River near Bethel showed evidence of corn having been planted in hills on about ten acres of cleared land.[10]

Wild River Valley remained little disturbed by indigenous peoples. Their numbers relative to territorial boundaries in the area, their social systems, and the state of their technology in hunting and gathering posed little threat to ecosystems in the river's watershed. In short, they tended to leave a light footprint on the land. While these factors are all important in assessing a culture's environmental effects, there is one that lies at the root of our relationship with the land and can have profound effects. It is how people feel about their place in the natural world; it is about the attitudes and values they hold, which, in turn, motivate their actions.

From archaeological discoveries, reports from encounters by early European explorers and settlers, oral and ceremonial traditions handed down through generations, and scientific descriptions of cultural groups and their customs, we are able to shed some light on their attitudes and values.[11] The key word that characterizes the environmental relationship of these indigenous peoples is "kinship" with other living and nonliving things in their surroundings. They saw themselves as one with the land, with social and spiritual obligations for the welfare of the rest of nature. This required a kind of proper community behavior—community in the sense that people were a part of the natural environment and related directly or indirectly to all things living and nonliving.

These values and perspectives, however, would be overrun before the end of the 1600s by events spelling the end of the independent way of life and thinking of the indigenous peoples of New England. It would be symbolized by the brutal King Philip's War of 1675–76, when the Wampanoag Chief Metacomet, also known as King Philip, was killed, beheaded, quartered, and displayed by the English in Rhode Island.[12]

The warning: Be good to those from away who have come to take your land and correct your slovenly, savage, and heathen ways or you will be punished.

For nearly another century, the Abenakis to the north resisted English expansion through a number of conflicts, but their efforts were doomed.[13] The Amarascoggins and the Pigwackets were able to hang on, probably as family bands, into the latter half of the 1700s, but by 1800 it appears that they, too, along with other bands of indigenous peoples, were gone from the upper Androscoggin.[14]

During that fateful time when the Amarascoggins were disappearing from the Wild River and upper Androscoggin region, the future of the valley was being influenced by degrees—literally. The events that set the stage for some of the changes to come in the valley were described in the late 1700s by the New Hampshire historian Jeremy Belknap, and it is likely that he himself would have found some of the consequences for the valley difficult to imagine. The key element that was about to be put in place in the mid to late 1700s in Wild River Valley was the boundary line between Maine and New Hampshire.

Setting boundaries between political divisions such as states is often made relatively easy by geographic features, and so it was initially with this boundary. All was well and good for the first forty miles or so as the line progressed northward up the middle of the Piscataqua River from Portsmouth Harbor, then up the Salmon Falls River to a small pond in its headwaters, today called Horn Pond in Wakefield, New Hampshire. Here, in 1740, according to Belknap, the English made a "royal determination" that "the dividing line was to run 'north, two degrees west, till one hundred and twenty miles were finished, from the mouth of Pascataqua harbour' . . . the extent of the Province of Maine."[15] However, the natural features of the land in some places beyond Horn Pond to the Canadian border were not clearly known, for large areas were still unexplored and not mapped sufficiently to give guidance. For example, Samuel Langdon's map of 1756 showed an expanse of land extending a distance below Umbagog Lake in the vicinity of Wild River Valley that he labeled "Wilderness unknown."[16]

The line's survey at the head of the Salmon Falls River was begun in

1741 by a surveyor who was given the order to allow ten degrees for the westerly variation (magnetic variation). Controversy over this survey led to another in 1768 and still another in 1789, the year New Hampshire became the ninth state admitted into the Union. With each survey, Belknap noted, the line changed, and today, it is not exactly straight but slightly bent.[17] The point here is that the final line, after all determinations were made, ended up bisecting Wild River Valley, and a difference of a few degrees one way or the other could have resulted in very different consequences regarding ownership and political and economic events that changed the valley. Even while the line was being determined during those early years, these events were beginning.

In 1772 the Commonwealth of Massachusetts, needing money because of the war with England, and desiring to encourage settlement of its wildlands in the District of Maine, granted 6,000 acres in the vicinity of the lower portion of Wild River Valley, including both sides of the Androscoggin River. Called the Peabody Patent, the land was sold for about $400.00, or 80 pounds, to Oliver and John Peabody and John and Samuel Bodwell.[18]

Other land investors soon followed in the early 1800s, buying the thousands of acres of public land that remained in the valley on both sides of the state line. Josiah Bachelder of Boston received a resolution from the General Court of the Commonwealth of Massachusetts in 1807 for a grant of land containing 28,882 acres in the District of Maine (Maine became a state in 1820) abutting the state line. The price was $4,803.66, but there was a hitch. Bachelder paid only $483.66, the remainder to be paid and the deed to be transferred to him only if within six years he had twenty families settled on his land. This did not occur until eleven years later. Nevertheless, he received his deed on June 22, 1816. Interestingly, his name had been misspelled as Batchelder on the original deed, as well as on all subsequent documents, so even today, maps still carry the name Batchelder's Grant.[19]

On May 22, 1832, Alpheus Bean purchased 33,000 acres that included most of the valley on the New Hampshire side, abutting Batchelder's Grant. Bean, then twenty-eight years of age, was a land speculator who had been born in Brownfield, Maine, and later moved to

Bartlett, New Hampshire, where he lived for many years.[20] The tract of land was named Bean's Purchase, a name that continues today on maps. Thus Wild River Valley experienced a shift in ownership, from public to private, and now entered the dreams of men who saw in the land a future for themselves.

At first, the impact of humans on the valley's ecological integrity occurred slowly. Nevertheless, groundwork, in a real sense, proceeded almost invisibly in concert with the sale of the land as surveyors penetrated the valley's deepest and most hidden recesses. These hardy men sighted lines, checked angles, measured distances, blazed trees, and set corners. Their work was transferred to maps and deeds, exchanged in law offices, further divided, inspected, sold, and translated into hopes and plans unimagined in the indigenous view that had prevailed for many thousands of years.

Among the first surveyors to arrive were those who marked out the Peabody Patent in 1791. Batchelder's Grant was laid out on the ground in 1807. Bean's Purchase was probably surveyed at various times in those early years because it is bordered not only by a state line, but by counties, townships, and other grants. Interestingly, the surveyors of the boundary of this grant were brought within a mile and a third of the old hemlock. At the point nearest to the hemlock, they undoubtedly had to move slowly and cautiously for they were on a steep slope. The view at an elevation 500 feet higher than the hemlock must have been spectacular as they looked out over the untouched forested valley.

Surveying was recognized as an honorable profession. A treatise published in the mid-1800s called it "perhaps the oldest of the mathematical arts . . . one of the most important at the present day, as determining the title to land, the foundation of the whole wealth of the world."[21] Surveying at that time was done mostly with a surveyor's chain and magnetic compass.[22] A Gunter's chain, invented by the Englishman Edmund Gunter, was used for measuring distances. The chain measured sixty-six feet, or four rods, in length and consisted of one hundred links. Each link was made of iron wire with a ring at each end connecting to the next link. Two or three rings were sometimes placed between links. Each link was exactly 7.92 inches long, including any rings in between.

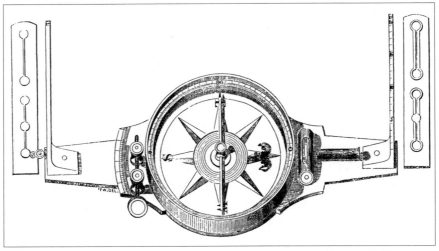

Compass used at the time of the early land surveying in Wild River Valley.
Reprinted from W. M. Gillespie, A Treatise on Land-Surveying,
8th ed. (New York: D. Appleton & Company, 1873), 126.

Eighty chains equaled one mile. Because each link with its associated links was one-hundredth of a chain, a distance less than a chain long could be measured by counting links and recording the distance as a decimal fraction of a chain, for example 6.35 chains meant six chains plus 35 links.

The compass was another important piece of equipment. It was invented in 1511 and consisted of two principal parts: a magnetic needle that pointed toward magnetic north and two vertical sights for determining the direction of the line being run. The problem of magnetic variation, or magnetic declination, the distance magnetic north varies from true north, made it difficult to resurvey lines with accuracy since the variation can change daily and annually and is influenced by the moon, solar storms, and nearby metal objects. In the latter half of the eighteenth century, instruments and techniques were developed to more easily calculate magnetic variation, and in the early nineteenth century, surveyors as a whole gradually began to accept the need to run true-north-based lines.

Surveyors encountering heavily wooded and rough terrain, like

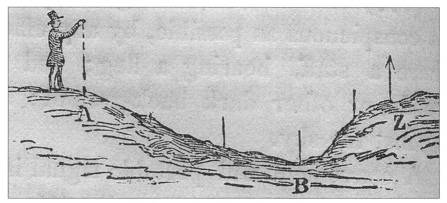

Early engraving of surveying a valley
Reprinted from W. M. Gillespie, A Treatise on Land-Surveying,
8th ed. (New York: D. Appleton & Company, 1873), 110.

Wild River Valley, found the work physically demanding. They worked in all kinds of weather, crossing steep slopes, deep ravines, swamps and wetlands, and thick woods. The work was also mentally demanding, especially in avoiding human error. They had to be accurate in sighting lines, measuring distances, and blazing trees to identify the line with as much exactness as they could muster. Measuring with the chain required two people—a forward chain man and a hind chain man, known as a leader and follower, respectively. One surveying text of the time advised that "the more careful and intelligent of [the] two . . . should generally be made the 'follower.'"[23] The two had to draw the chain tightly and check for kinks and bent links. On steep hills, they often used only half or a quarter of a chain at a time in order to keep it level. All of these measuring activities required accurate counting of chains and links with records kept in a field book. Blazes on trees were cut with axes to show whether a tree was directly on the line or to one side or the other and how far from the line. Corners needed to be marked accurately and prominently. Thus Wild River Valley was marked and divided and readied for those who would come to make a living off the land and begin to fracture the ecological continuity and pattern that had developed over millennia.

Settlers arrived slowly. Some of the first came via the old Native, or

Pigwacket, trail through Evans Notch and settled along the Androscoggin River in the vicinity of the Peabody Patent. In 1778 one settler was killed by Indian marauders, and by 1791 only one settler was present in the Peabody Patent. However, by 1804, twenty families had arrived, and in that year, they successfully petitioned the Massachusetts Legislature to incorporate the town of Gilead.[24]

A road planned by the owner of Batchelder's Grant in 1832 was to follow the Pigwacket Trail from Fryeburg to Gilead, but a century would pass before it was completed. That owner was Ellis B. Usher, who began buying up Batchelder's Grant in 1826 after the death of Josiah Bachelder. Usher was one of the largest lumber dealers and wildland owners in Maine. By 1832 he owned 13,000 acres.[25] Still, Wild River Valley remained essentially absent of settlement during the first half of the nineteenth century. In 1860 the United States Census noted only one settler in the Wild River Valley. Those who visited it were, for the most part, a few loggers and people who hunted, trapped, and fished, so most of the valley remained relatively untouched and peacefulness reigned around the old hemlock.

From early times, wild areas drew people in search of wildlife for food and fur, and Wild River Valley was no different—although, as the logging historian William Gove pointed out, early accounts mentioned an almost complete lack of deer and other wildlife in thick, virgin forests that characterized areas such as the valley.[26] As settlement and logging progressed, however, openings produced browse for many species, including deer and other game animals. Hunting and fishing were necessary to settlers for putting food on the table, and bear, moose, deer, grouse, ducks, and fish were all sought after. When the Atlantic & St. Lawrence opened in 1851 for traffic from Portland, Maine, to Gilead, more people came to hunt and fish for recreation. Gilead farmers rented rooms to them, and many built hunting camps in the valley.[27] The valley was to remain popular for fishing and hunting throughout the years. A report in 1891 told of fishing parties passing through Gilead "for Wild river every day."[28] *The Mountaineer*, a Gorham, New Hampshire, weekly, reported in 1890: "Hunters from South Paris [Maine] brought out five deer from Wild River to-day."[29] At the turn of the century, in

1901, the journalist L. C. Bateman, writing for the *Lewiston Journal*, went into the valley on a hunting trip. He later reported that deer, bear, and bobcat were in abundance and "the skilful [*sic*] hunter is rarely obliged to return empty handed from his quest."[30]

During the 1800s the growing population in America began to look more carefully at other resources of the land. Many states authorized and conducted scientific surveys, often headed up by geologists and naturalists. Of special interest were the wildlands about which little was known. The geologist Charles H. Hitchcock was prominent in scientific expeditions in both Maine and New Hampshire in the second half of the nineteenth century. As early as 1874, his first report on the geology of New Hampshire noted, "A considerable tributary, Wild River, rises in Bean's Purchase, but flows into the Androscoggin in Maine."[31]

Hitchcock's second report, published in 1877, gives a geologist's view of the valley and its Evans Brook arm as they existed before the virgin forest was stripped away:

The great area of country stretching southward from the Androscoggin river in Shelburne is for miles a wilderness, uninhabited save by the denizens of the forests. It is broken by hills and valleys, rock cliffs and deep gorges, mountain ridges and precipitous slopes; while on the west side of Bean's Purchase, and on the state line near Chatham, we have mountains that rise to the height of nearly four thousand feet. . . . The gorge between Mts. Wildcat and Carter is quite remarkable as any among the mountains, especially its southern opening. The precipitous wall of rock on the west, the overhanging cliffs on the east, the great mass of *debris* across the valley that confines the water of a small lake, are all of intense interest to the geologist. On the east the Bricket notch, just over the border in Maine, is remarkable; particularly in the way in which the streams divide as they come down from the side of the Notch. The stream from Mt. Royce, where it leaves the steep slope of the mountain, divides; a part runs north into the Androscoggin, and the rest flows into the Saco. But what is most wonderful, from Speckled mountain, on the south-east side of the Notch, there is a stream the exact counterpart of the one from Mt. Royce;—so that the height of land in the Notch is an island by being surrounded by water from these two streams, or rather four streams, after the two have divided. At the head waters of the east branch of the Saco there is a low notch towards Wild river, and the slopes of the sides are regular compared to most notches about these mountains.[32]

Mining was among the strong economic motives that lay behind the interests of states in sponsoring the scientific surveys. Mining, however, was never of more than minor importance in this region of the White Mountains; for example, gold mining has never been reported.[33] A mineral investigation of 27,000 aces of the Bean's Purchase section of the valley concluded that, although none were found, "small amounts of beryl and possibly tourmaline of gemstone or specimen quality may exist in the study area."[34] Historic records indicate quarries just outside the valley's watershed. At least one is close to the watershed's divide near the top of North Baldface Mountain at the southern end of the valley and is reported as a collecting site for gem-quality beryl crystals found in pegmatite. Pegmatite is a coarse-grained igneous rock containing feldspar, quartz, "books" of mica, and crystals of minerals such as garnet, tourmaline, and beryl. The North Baldface quarry may be the one referred to in the New Hampshire geological report of 1877: ". . . on the east side of Baldface a granite has been quarried that contains quite a large proportion of feldspar."[35] Limited deposits of pegmatite have been discovered in outcrops of various sizes elsewhere in the valley.[36] Although lead, zinc, silver, and tin have been mined from rocks north and south of the valley, they are thought to be of low economic significance in the valley along with construction materials such as dimension and crushed stone.[37]

While hunting, trapping, fishing, mining, and clearing the land for homes and farms, by themselves, initially posed no serious threat to the ecological balance in the valley and the old hemlock's surroundings, not so logging. At first, lumbering around Wild River occurred near the settlement of Gilead at the north end of the old Indian trail and south of Evans Notch and Batchelder's Grant in Cold River Valley. Near Gilead, large old-growth white pines were logged in these early years. In nearby

Bean's Purchase, there is little record of logging until the early 1860s, with perhaps the exception of trespass logging in which people cut trees on land they didn't own. However, arrival of the railroad in 1851 set off a series of actions that would change Wild River Valley forever by providing an alternative to the river-driving method of getting the logs to the mills and to growing markets for lumber and wood products closer to the coast.[38]

The presence of the railroad probably stimulated one of Maine's largest mill owners and lumber dealers to turn his eye toward the timber wealth of Wild River Valley. His name was Joseph Hobson, and he began buying up Bean's Purchase in 1853. By 1859 he owned it all. Hobson's ownership combined with Usher's, who owned thousands of acres of Batchelder's Grant, prompted the historian D. B. Wight to comment: "Now that the great virgin forest of Wild River was owned almost entirely by two of the largest lumber dealers in Maine, Ellis Usher and Joseph Hobson, there was danger of the forest being raped and destroyed by the crude and wasteful lumbering methods used in those days."[39] This would prove to be true.

The lumbermen faced a major problem: getting the logs out of the valley to the railroad. The choice was driving them down the river or hauling them over woods roads. Hauling, which was then carried out mostly by oxen, was long and time-consuming. Driving required dams to flush the logs down, but the boulder-packed bed of the river made driving difficult, and the uncontrollable force of the mountain river during ice-out and spring runoff was already well known. The lumbermen, however, chose to build dams and drive the logs down the river, but by the end of 1860, they had learned firsthand the river's destructive force: a number of dams and mills had been lost.[40]

In 1851 the name Hastings first appeared in the history of Wild River Valley. David Robinson (Rob) Hastings was born in 1823 in Bethel, Maine, studied law, became a county attorney, and served in the Civil War. He was active in the Democratic Party at the national level. His outside business interests included timberlands and lumbering.[41] So it was not out of character for him to have purchased land in the nearby valley.[42]

*David R. "Rob" Hastings was a lawyer and businessman
who purchased land in Wild River Valley in 1851 for timber harvesting. The land included the future site of the
logging village of Hastings, Maine. Reprinted from
William B. Lapham, comp.,* History of Bethel, Formerly
Sudbury Canada, 1768–1890 *(Augusta, ME: Press of the
Maine Farmer, 1891), 376a.*

The purchase included a key piece of land, one that would be connected to the profound change in the natural world to which the old
hemlock was connected. The property was a level, fertile piece of about
150 to 200 acres containing deep, rich alluvial soil and located in the triangle between Evans Brook and Wild River immediately south of their
confluence. It was described at the time as an intervale "containing excel-
lent tillage land."[43] Because it had been difficult to get to, no permanent
settlement existed before the purchase. At the end of 1859, Hastings and

Gideon A. Hastings, with his brother David R., was a large landowner of Batchelder's Grant in Wild River Valley who spent many years in the lumber business in the valley. Reprinted from William B. Lapham, comp., History of Bethel, Formerly Sudbury Canada, 1768–1890 *(Augusta, ME: Press of the Maine Farmer, 1891), 560a.*

a partner completed the construction of a sawmill and dam on the river and employed about fifty men cutting in the area.[44]

In 1864 David R. Hastings moved his law office to Fryeburg on the south side of Evans Notch, but apparently this did not diminish his interest in Wild River Valley timber.[45] Six years later, he and his two brothers, John Decatur (Cate) Hastings and Major Gideon Alfonso Hastings, began buying up land in Batchelder's Grant.[46] Of the three, Gideon became perhaps the most prominent in the events that followed and so greatly influenced Wild River Valley. He also had learned the black-smith trade from his father, but he had wider interests, especially in business. Gideon had been drawn to the lumber business early in his career but interrupted it by enlisting in the army in 1861 to take part in the Civil War. He commanded the Twelfth Maine Regiment in the battles of Baton Rouge and Irish Bend. In 1863 he was promoted to major, a title that he held the rest of his life. Following his discharge from service in 1866, he became a successful plantation owner in the South, but due to malaria he returned to Maine, where he began a long association with the timberlands of Batchelder's Grant.[47]

By the 1880s Gideon and David Hastings had acquired 14,000 acres, John having dropped out of the venture. Early in that decade, Gideon built a farm on the intervale land by Wild River and Evans Brook. The farm served as the headquarters for his logging operations.[48] The year 1883 found the Hastings brothers were expanding their business enterprise, and in that year participated in a purchase of land on the Shelburne, New Hampshire, side of the valley, extending from the Bean's Purchase boundary up to the valley's ridgeline.[49]

The valley at this time was still relatively untouched. Evidence of lumbering in the main valley of Wild River on the New Hampshire side consisted of early cuttings and the remains of an old dam or two, but the upper valley still appeared "wild and desolate."[50] A view of the valley in 1883 seen by an Appalachian Mountain Club (AMC) party from the summit of East Royce Mountain revealed a "broad, dark wilderness, cheered by an occasional gleam of the boulder-strewn Wild River sweeping out to the Androscoggin intervale." To the east were "the fine forms of Caribou and Speckled Mountain. . . ."[51] And down below, beneath the beauty and grandeur of the "bold cliff structure of Mt. Royce," only three miles from Major Hastings' farm, a logging road turned to a trail through Evans Notch—"a narrow, forest-shaded tract . . . bordered by banks of trailing arbutus, dalibarda [dewdrop of the rose family], and other growths."[52]

On January 16 of that same year, 1883, a Gilead item in the *Oxford Democrat* noted: "Major Hastings is doing an extensive business on Wild River—500 cords of bark were landed near the railroad . . . 150,000 cords of spruce landed on Wild River."[53] And of course the hemlock trees themselves were logged and sold. Based on the depletion rate of hemlock trees supplying bark to large tanneries in Maine, this could translate into the removal of hemlock from 1,600 acres.[54] These would have been virgin trees, like the old hemlock tree on the other side of the valley. They represented hundreds of years of slow growth and development to maturity and the establishment of ecological relationships with the soil, microclimate, and plants and animals, many symbiotic, or mutually beneficial. All these characteristics of a healthy ecosystem were being destroyed or severely interrupted by the loggers and bark hunters.

In their defense, the forest in those days was seen as a vast, nearly unlimited resource, and the ecological benefits of the woodland, including its hemlock trees, were little known, and there was little common awareness and understanding of what *was* known. The benefit of hemlock *bark,* to the contrary, was well known. Tanning of leather, that is, making animal skins tough, pliable, and long-lasting, was a process that had great economic value. Tannins are chemicals that produce these qualities in hides when they are used in the process of tanning. The bark of the eastern hemlock tree is a primary source of tannin with a content of 10 to 12 percent.[55] As such, it was centrally involved in the production of necessary leather goods of the time—"harness, saddlery, traces, belts for wheels, boots and shoes, and similar articles made of leather, but also vests, doublets, and breeches for men and jerkins, petticoats, and aprons for women," among other products.[56] This demand for leather goods and the presence of large quantities of tanbark were among the factors that contributed to the rise of the industry in Maine.

At about the time when Major Hastings' men were harvesting hemlock bark, Maine's tanning industry had risen to national importance and was the state's second-ranking industry in dollar value.[57] In fact, the industry was at its peak, and hemlock bark was in great demand. For example, in 1870, 63,470 cords of hemlock bark, selling at an average price of $6.75 per cord, were needed to feed the industry.[58] Two and one-half cords of bark were needed to tan one hundred hides.[59]

We only have figures for one year of bark cutting by Major Hastings' crews, but it is likely that this was a business Hastings conducted for sev-

Leon Leonwood (L. L.) Bean (on left) and his cousin and hunting companion, Louvie Swett — 1897. L. L. Bean's first hunting trip was in Wild River Valley with his cousin.
PHOTOGRAPH COURTESY OF L. L. BEAN, INC.

eral years. The old hemlock escaped this threat because it grew in Bean's Purchase, not on land owned by the Hastings brothers. Up to this time, the loggers had been limited by technology and economic efficiency to cutting within a reasonable distance from the road and the river. Most of the valley's mature ecological systems and its rich natural diversity were still intact, including its wildlife. Reports of white-tailed deer and black bear, even woodland caribou, were circulated in the 1880s.[60] These attracted hunters, not only those who logged the area but outsiders who came for the sport of hunting.

One visitor, who arrived in the valley to hunt in 1885, would come to exert an enormous, though indirect, influence on many of those who sought out the valley in the next century for outdoor recreational pursuits. His name was Leon Leonwood Bean (no relationship to the Bean of Bean's Purchase).[61] At the early age of thirteen and an orphan, he arrived at Major Hastings' farm on his first hunting trip and fell in love with the valley.

L. L. Bean's camp in Wild River Valley. L. L. Bean made many annual hunting trips into Wild River Valley in the late 1800s and early 1900s. He stayed in the office building of the logging camp that he used on his first trip. The company that owned the building allowed him to repair and use it. Bean named the camp Dew Drop Inn.
PHOTOGRAPH COURTESY OF L. L. BEAN, INC.

Bean came back the next year with a cousin and stayed in an old lumbering camp just over the New Hampshire line in Bean's Purchase. His cousin shot a deer on their second day and went home. Bean later wrote that the night his cousin left him alone at the camp was "the longest and most dismal of my life."[62] The next day he shot a large buck. He stayed nearly two weeks at the camp, sold his deer for twelve dollars to two unsuccessful hunters, and set out a trapline, from which he caught four sables and one wild cat.

The hunting trips hooked Bean, and for many years he made up hunting parties and returned to stay in the logging camp office. In 1901 he offered to buy the camp, but the lumber company refused to sell it,

(Left to right) L. L. Bean and his brothers Ortho and Guy Bean. In the winter of 1923 L. L. and his brothers vacationed at Dew Drop Inn and tested snowshoes.
PHOTOGRAPH COURTESY OF L. L. BEAN, INC.

instead allowing him to repair and use it. Bean named the camp Dew Drop Inn and hunted out of it for more than thirty years, shooting many deer. The trips spawned in Bean an interest in finding comfortable outdoor footwear, and in 1911 he invented his famous hunting shoe. This led to the establishment of his world-renowned firm, L. L. Bean, in Freeport, Maine.

One hundred years later, in the spring of 1985, L. L. Bean's grandson, Leon Gorman, then head of the great enterprise of outdoor wear and recreational equipment his grandfather founded, hiked along the northwest rim of Wild River Valley with the executive director of the AMC. As he stood gazing down into his grandfather's old hunting grounds, he was informed that the AMC wanted to preserve the area below as wilderness.[63] Such a thought would have been inconceivable to those L. L. Bean had met at Major Hastings' lumbering headquarters during his hunting trip. That was a time when the valley was seen through other eyes, and only a matter of time before those eyes would multiply and swarm into the valley, seeing only its timber. And amazingly, at least one old hemlock would survive as a living witness.

Three

Cutting Lifelines

Through the 1800s, while the old hemlock stood silent and undisturbed on its hillside, human activity accelerated on the triangle of intervale land between Evans Brook and Wild River. With his farm established and producing oats and potatoes, and with his logging and sawmill operations growing, Major Gideon Hastings had big plans. For the ambitious, success breeds ideas and forward movement overcomes distant dreams. Major Hastings saw a future at Wild River—a bright future for a woods business of logging timber for lumber, stock for wood-turning mills and other products, and bark for tanneries. As a result, the last half of the 1880s was an increasingly busy time at the Hastings farm, woods operations, and mill. Gideon and his son, David Robinson Hastings, ran the business. David was named after his uncle, Gideon's brother "Rob," who continued as a partner in the business while involved in his law practice and politics. The Hastings family business was alone in the valley, and the enterprise progressed smoothly and quite predictably. But if anything is predictable, it's change itself, and a big change had been brewing that would leave its impact on the valley for the next century or more.

While the Hastings family business had been growing, a series of events of a much quieter nature, yet with more profound consequences, had been taking place, all involving the sale of Bean's Purchase. On June 13, 1883, a clerk recorded the following in Volume 12, page 2, in the Registry of Deeds for Coos County, New Hampshire: "Joseph Hobson sold Bean's Purchase for $50,500.00 to Charles E. Dole and Simon J. Murphy." This transaction, by itself, did not change anything in the valley. Eight months later, on February 22, 1884, a clerk in the same registry recorded that Dole and Murphy turned around and sold one-third of their interest in Bean's Purchase to a George Fuller.[1] Still

Samuel D. Hobson
From Hamilton Child, Gazetteer of Caledonia and
Essex Counties, Vermont, 1764–1887 *(Syracuse, NY:*
Syracuse Journal Co., Printers and Binders, 1887).

nothing happened. No new logging occurred up in Wild River Valley, and the sale seemed to draw no notice.

Then on June 24, 1890, Dole and Murphy sold their remaining two-thirds interest in Wild River Valley to Samuel Decatur Hobson.[2] The other one-third was also acquired by Hobson from the widow of George Fuller. It appeared that Hobson now owned all of Bean's Purchase—the whole New Hampshire side of Wild River Valley. Hobson then sold one-half of the land to Eben C. Robinson and George H. Fitzgerald.[3] All were from Island Pond, Vermont, a village in Brighton located in the Northeast Kingdom. Interestingly, in 1780, Brighton had the name "Gilead," the same as Gilead, Maine. The Vermont State Legislature changed the name to Brighton in 1832.[4]

Hobson was a Maine man born in Hollis in 1830. He grew up on a farm, graduated from Limerick Academy, and at the age of twenty began learning the carpentry trade. In 1852 he moved to Island Pond and eventually managed a mill and lumber business. Later, he became a land agent, United States Customs officer, legislator, and assistant judge. His source of income came from a business he established manufacturing building lumber, clapboards, shingles, laths, and other products. While Hobson was the principal owner and took the lead in developing and managing the Wild River Valley investment, his partners were also active businessmen. Fitzgerald owned the Fitzgerald Land and Lumber Company in Brighton, a leading private industry which was bringing much prosperity to the area. Robinson was listed with both Hobson and Fitzgerald in an 1891 gazetteer as grain dealers and shippers associated with the Central Vermont Railway System, which, in turn, was connected to the Grand Trunk Railway System that passed through Gilead, Maine. One reporter wrote that they were "some of the best known business men in northern Vermont."[5]

The interest that these entrepreneurs had in Wild River Valley, of course, was its timber. Some assessment of the valley's natural character and economic value at the time comes from a correspondent with experience in such matters:

Bean's Purchase is primitive forest, consisting of a heavy growth of spruce and pine timber, also some very fine white birch. From an experience in the examination and exploration of timber land in all parts of New England and the British Provinces during the last 25 years, I submit my judgment in regard to Bean's Purchase. The town contains in the close vicinity of 200,000,000 ft. of timber as good as any on the Connecticut and Penobscot rivers, and on account of its ease of access by and to railroads, its accessibility to all of the eastern lumber markets, I consider it one of the most valuable tracts of primitive timber land in New England to-day.[6]

That fall into December, a series of news items traced the preliminary activities of the company. Near the end of September, Gorham,

New Hampshire's weekly, *The Mountaineer*, reported that "S. D. Hobson is to put up a new mill on Wild River above the opening [Hastings' intervale land at Evans Brook] this fall; there will be more logging than last winter we understand, so all together we are looking for a big winter's work in our little town."[7] This last statement only hints at the tremendous excitement and anticipation the townspeople of Gilead must have felt, for as Hugh Chapman and Howard Reiche, historians of the Gilead Historical Society, pointed out, the enterprises of Hastings and Hobson were integral to the economic and social well-being of Gilead: "All the forest products . . . had to go through Gilead or be used by the Gilead mills. . . . Gilead flourished with stores, mills, numerous boarding houses, farms for hay and vegetables, a multi-track railroad yard, blacksmiths. . . ."[8]

Hastings, Maine — 1890s. View looking southwest from The Roost. Evans Brook and Notch are on the left, and the main valley of Wild River is on the right.

By the end of October, the new company had taken the name Wild River Lumber Company (although it wouldn't be incorporated until the next June), and Hobson had brought in thirty to fifty men who had cleared land and put up a mill about two and a half miles above the opening. Plans were made to build two more mills—one opposite the Hastings family mill and another three miles above the mill already constructed upriver from the opening. In early November a boiler was

Wild River Railroad and Hastings, Maine— 1895.
Reprinted from Map of Oxford County, Maine—1895.

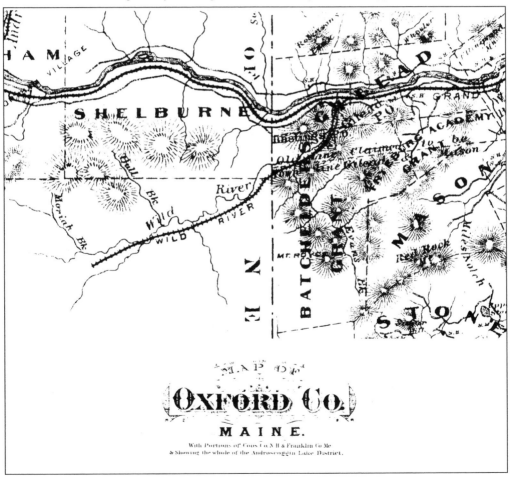

hauled up to the new mill, and on December 5, the mill began sawing boards. To feed the mill, loggers and horses were needed, and by mid-December, more than fifty horses had been brought in and plans were to work a hundred or more in the coming winter.[9]

The first of May the next year, 1891, a party of engineers for the Wild River Lumber Company began exploring the valley for the route of a logging railroad to open up the land for timber harvesting, and by July 1 an unbelievable amount of progress had been made. Nine miles of the railway route had been located and most of it surveyed, and a contract had been signed with a builder for completion of the section by November 1 of that same year. The surveys showed that the grade of the railroad averaged only 52 feet per mile, "everything the company could wish." Twenty-five Italian workers were already on site grading the line and preparing ties. The Hastings family business had sold rights to some of its intervale land at the opening to the Wild River Lumber Company for roads, railway sidings, and mill buildings and yards, and the new company already had crews digging and cutting stone for the foundations of a long-lumber mill and a boardinghouse. The company's mill, built the previous year upriver, had begun sawing lumber for the construction of buildings, culverts, trestles, and other structures. The Hastings family enterprise had signed an agreement with the company that the Hastings mills would be connected to the company's railroad tracks, and that their manufactured lumber would be hauled at an agreed-upon price to the Grand Trunk Railway in Gilead. The Hastings business also was making plans to move its own mill up Evans Brook with a spur track leading to it.[10]

By the end of August 1891 a large boardinghouse, a store, and a company office were under construction, and work on the mill was soon to start.[11] Then a setback occurred: that fall, the company's upper mill burned.[12] The brook near the mill was later named Burnt Mill Brook. *The Mountaineer* also reported an unfortunate accident at a railroad construction site: "One of the Italians was badly hurt . . . by a rail flying and hitting him in the face."[13] Nevertheless, in October the railroad track was finished about halfway up to the new mill.[14] Also that fall it was reported that the company had two railroad engines and had sold white birch

Hastings Village looking southwest — 1890s
PHOTOGRAPH COURTESY OF THE UNITED STATES FOREST SERVICE,
WHITE MOUNTAIN NATIONAL FOREST

stumpage to a firm.[15] As soon as the railroad was up and running, it began hauling the sawlogs.[16]

By mid-November, *The Mountaineer* reported that the "opening is getting to be quite a little village."[17] Not all proceeded smoothly, however. In December a train went off the track.[18] The unfortunate event would be the first of many railroad accidents to plague the company during its operation. On a good note, however, the Wild River Lumber Company successfully installed a telephone line from its mill in the valley to the company's office in Gilead.[19]

Hastings Village looking southwest — 1890s
PHOTOGRAPH COURTESY OF THE UNITED STATES FOREST SERVICE,
WHITE MOUNTAIN NATIONAL FOREST

During this year of 1891, Gideon Hastings' brother Rob sold his half interest in the enterprise to his partner, Gideon, and nephew and namesake, David Robinson Hastings, Gideon's son. The name of the business was changed to G. A. and D. R. Hastings—father and son. Eventually the company acquired all of Batchelder's Grant—a tract of land of more than 25,000 acres.[20]

In 1892 the new community took shape, complete with a post office that had opened in February. That same month, a news item in *The Mountaineer* referred to the village as Hastings, named by the Wild River Lumber Company in honor of Major Hastings.[21] A note said that passengers were using the train from Hastings to Gilead at a fare of fifteen cents.[22] That summer, six small homes were built by the Wild River Lumber Company, and for those families with children, a schoolteacher

*Gideon A. Hastings after whom Hastings Village was
named. In this photograph, Major Hastings is about
seventy-five years old. Photograph reprinted from the*
Bethel News, *Wednesday, June 10, 1896.*

was hired. She was Jennie Rich of Bethel, a much admired, successful, and experienced teacher.[23]

At the end of September, the Wild River Lumber Company mill, which had been up and running, was temporarily shut down, probably for repairs or installation of new machinery, and was scheduled to reopen on November 1. The company had started construction of an extension of the railroad to the headwaters of Moriah Brook with a very steep grade of 317 feet per mile. David Hastings had started extensive repairs on his mill, putting in better machinery and building more spur track to haul logs in to his millpond. Houses for his employees also were under construction.[24]

By 1894 several hundred men were employed by the company.[25] The

Sawmill of the Wild River Lumber Company— 1890s.
Lumber was the lifeblood of the village of Hastings.

Barn at Hastings, Maine— 1890s

late Ralph Peabody, a resident of nearby Shelburne, New Hampshire, described the community as a whole village with a schoolhouse, store, boardinghouse, barn, and many cottages for mill men to live in.[26] Another resident was Gard Bennett, who was only a child when his father ran a locomotive on the logging railroad. He said years later that "in Hastings there were 11 houses, a boardinghouse located on Wild River, three houses in another place, and 5 houses on Smokey Row. There was a school house, a general store, Post Office, saw mill, and engine house."[27] According to another historical account, "a row of ten five-room houses boasted electric lights, a tub in every other house, and running water from a nearby spring. Electricity was supplied by a steam-operated dynamo at the sawmill."[28]

Through the 1890s, the town flourished and developed a social life in keeping with that of rural villages throughout this mountainous region. Over the years, the school had several teachers, at least one from

The "Ten Commandments" and company store—1890s. The row houses for workers and their families are situated along the edge of Wild River. The Roost is in the background.
PHOTOGRAPH COURTESY OF THE BETHEL HISTORICAL SOCIETY

each of the nearby communities of Bethel, Maine, and Gorham, New Hampshire. The store, of course, was a place where people frequently came, not only for the wide range of goods—from clothing to food—that it stocked, but for their mail, as the post office was at one end. The store also attracted workmen in the evening who caught up on their experiences of the day. The boardinghouse held as many as fifty men who worked in the woods and mills. Many were of French and Irish heritage, but many other nationalities were represented—Russians, Swedes, Germans, Austrians, Danes, and Yankees. They were hardworking and eager to enjoy hearty meals. Beans were a staple, cooked in a bean hole outside the boardinghouse. The company's sawmill started at 6:00 A.M. and ran for twelve hours, so an early breakfast started the working day.[29]

Despite the long days and hard labor, the residents also found time for enjoyment. On Saturday evenings, dances were held at the boardinghouse or in Gilead, and the sound of music from accordions, harmonicas, and fiddles floated up through the valley. Another social affair was the community Christmas tree held at the schoolhouse on Christmas Eve when presents were given and received. There were times when alcohol made its way into some of the festivities and caused a few absences from the next morning's breakfast and a few bruises from fights. Rum, for example, shared the blame one August day when a blacksmith's hammer effectively settled an argument with a blow to a skull leaving a mind insensible. But overall, one newspaper reported, "the people are industrious and peaceful."[30]

The forest, of course, was the heart of the village's prosperity, and the mills added to its value. None of the mills was particularly unusual except for one, perhaps the only one of its kind in Maine. Sometime during these early years at Hastings, Wild River Lumber Company introduced a wood alcohol plant to the community.[31] Most of these chemical plants were located in states with large areas of hardwood, such as those in New York, New Jersey, Pennsylvania, West Virginia, Tennessee, Ohio, and Michigan. By 1890 alcohol plants had operated in the country for many years, and the industry and its processes had become well established. These plants, including the one at Hastings, produced methyl alcohol, also known as methanol, as well as acetate of lime and charcoal.

Company Store at Hastings, Maine — 1890s. The store also housed the post office.
PHOTOGRAPH COURTESY OF THE MAINE HISTORIC PRESERVATION COMMISSION

Boardinghouse and part of the mill crew at Hastings, Maine — 1890s
PHOTOGRAPH COURTESY OF THE MAINE HISTORIC PRESERVATION COMMISSION

Oxen and loggers in Wild River Valley

Basically, the manufacturing process, known as *destructive* distillation, involves heating hardwood in the absence of oxygen up to 600 degrees Fahrenheit. Gases are driven off from the wood and drawn through coolers and condensers to produce methyl alcohol and acetic acid, which is reacted with lime to make acetate of lime. In the process, the remaining wood is turned into charcoal.

The plant at Hastings utilized seasoned hard maple, birch, and beech cut into four-foot lengths. Workers brought the wood in from outdoors where it was stored. At times, there were as many as 4,000 cords piled up outside the plant. The wood was hand-loaded into airtight metal retorts, cast iron or steel cylinders 60 inches in diameter and 112 inches long. Each held about three-quarters of a cord of wood, a cord being four feet high by four feet deep by eight feet long. Gard Bennett said that the alcohol mill had twelve furnaces, which meant that they had twelve retorts over them with the capacity to distill nine cords of wood at a time. Whether this was before the plant was overhauled is not clear. A complete run could be made in about twelve hours.

During the process the vapors were piped into a water-cooled condenser and from there into a settling tank to remove tar. Then the liquid was distilled further to remove dissolved tar and produce water, acetic acid, and methanol. Lime was added, which combined with the acid. Heat drove off the methanol, after which it was condensed, barreled, and shipped to a refinery. The product was in much demand at the time as a solvent. The remaining liquid acetate of lime was passed on to drying pans where it was evaporated, raked, and turned by hand until it produced gray crystals of acetate of lime. The product was then bagged and shipped. Acetate of lime was utilized by industries using chemicals for the manufacture of such products as dyes and textiles. The charcoal was removed and cooled and most likely used as fuel for the furnaces.

The Wild River Railroad, which fed the mills during these busy years, continued to push up into the valley, giving access to its vast wealth of timber. Spurs of various lengths continued to be built up the river's major tributaries, and eventually included Bull, Moriah, Blue, Cypress, and Spruce Brooks. The railroad terminated at Logging Camp No. 9, stopping short of No Ketchum Pond and Perkins Notch in the upper reaches of Wild River's headwaters. At its completion, the railroad, from its junction with the Grand Trunk Railway in Gilead, extended fifteen miles up the valley, and a total of another five miles of spur-line tracks were laid up the river's tributary streams. Many bridges were required to traverse the rough country, and a long, spectacular trestle spanned Moriah Brook Gorge.[32] Slowly, with the advance of the railroad, the steep hillsides of the valley were disrobed of their verdant clothing and left naked and bare to the elements.

The expansion of the railroad was a key element in the growth of the village and in the intensification of logging and mill activity in the valley. When the railroad had pushed up along the river and by the mouth of Blue Brook, the crack and thump of axes and sledges moved ever closer to the old hemlock. And when a spur line in the vicinity of the brook

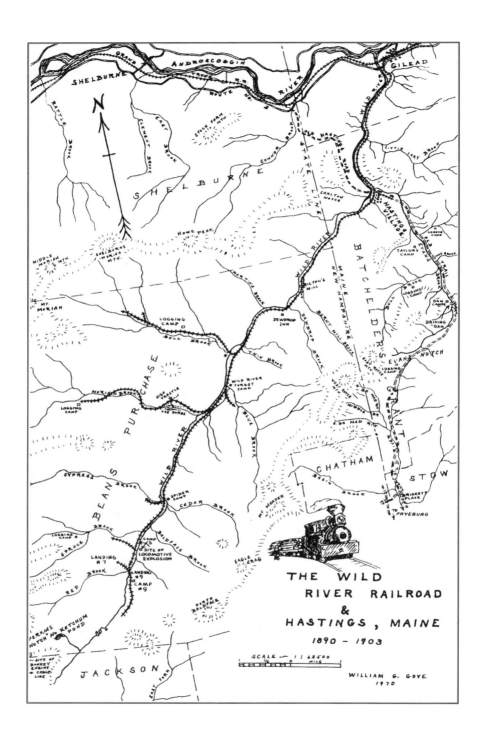

THE WILD
RIVER RAILROAD
&
HASTINGS, MAINE
1890 – 1903

SCALE – 1 : 62500
MILE

WILLIAM G. GOVE
1970

Above: Logging yard in Wild River Valley
PHOTOGRAPH COURTESY OF THE UNITED STATES FOREST SERVICE,
WHITE MOUNTAIN NATIONAL FOREST
Left: The Wild River Railroad and Hastings, Maine—1890–1903
MAP COURTESY OF WILLIAM G. GOVE

crept toward the great tree, the air around the tree undoubtedly pulsated with the distant sounds, and vibrations perhaps even reached its broad, shallow root structure. But the tree was never reached. Why? It would be more than a century later before we would be better able to answer this question.

Different kinds of locomotives were employed on the railroad. The Shay locomotive was a favorite among lumbering and mining companies where railroad beds were rough, steep, and twisting. This was a slow-moving, noisy engine with a patented drive mechanism that utilized vertical cylinders on one side with a special gear arrangement. It was this

Above: The Gilead, Shay Engine #1, of the Wild River Railroad.
The Shay engines were the workhorses on the logging railroads. They hauled
log trains up steep grades and over rough, twisting roadbeds.
Below: A Shay engine hauling a log train near Hastings, Maine—1890s.

Wild River Railroad bridge across Evans Brook at Hastings, Maine
PHOTOGRAPH COURTESY OF THE MAINE HISTORIC PRESERVATION COMMISSION

locomotive that ran up to the cutting operations in the valley. As the logs were cut by double-bitted axes and crosscut saws, they were taken down the steep slopes by horse and sled to sidings where they were rolled onto the log cars and hauled to the mills. Another locomotive was used to make runs twice a day to Gilead hauling flatcars loaded with lumber from the mills and a car carrying both freight and passengers.[33]

The railroad was vulnerable to the elements and suffered from flooding, washouts, and landslides, as well as accidents from mechanical problems. On April 11, 1894, *The Mountaineer* reported that a log train coming out of the woods "ran away, killing the engineer and one break [*sic*] hand who was on the logs."[34] Then again on November 14 that same year, a train coming down to Gilead "left the track and tipped on its side. Two traveling men . . . were badly scalded and one received a broken arm. The accident was caused, so the engineer said, by a chain falling from the front of the engine under the wheels."[35]

The next year, 1895, the valley experienced an ominous sign of things to come. Dark, sinister fingers of smoke drifted up Blue Brook and crept up the ridge where the old hemlock stood. As the smoke thickened, a dark, yellowish haze enveloped the valley. Two miles away, across the river in the area of Moriah and Bull Brooks, a fire swiftly snaked through slash piles of cut-off treetops and limbs left by the loggers. One report called it the first large fire in logging slash in the White Mountain National Forest. When it was over, 4,960 acres stood naked and black. But the fire never jumped Wild River, and the old hemlock was untouched.[36]

The logging community took these ups and downs in stride, but on February 22, 1898, an item appeared in the *Oxford Democrat* that surely captured the interest of the village residents:

> The Wild River Lumber Company property was sold to a syndicate. . . . The Company has operated in Hastings for the last seven years. They constructed a railroad from Gilead and on their property had a mill, a store, a boarding house, shops, and twenty or more dwellings. The Wild River Lumber Company owned lands in Maine and 48,000 acres in New Hampshire. Business will henceforth be continued under the new company on a larger scale.[37]

The new company was named Hastings Lumber Company, although the Hastings family was not connected with it. The *Maine Register* for the years 1898–99 lists Daniel F. Emery, Jr., of Portland as president of the company.[38] Hastings Lumber Company continued the work of its predecessor, heavily logging the valley's slopes and keeping the locomotives busily hauling to the mills. In 1899 six logging camps operated up in the valley engaging the work of about three hundred men.[39]

The logging operations of the new company, however, were not without incident, and a terrible one soon occurred. On April 19, 1899, the *Bethel News* reported: "One of the engines of the Hastings Lumber Company at Hastings blew up yesterday afternoon near Camp No. 1, and killed three men instantly. One of the men was said to have been blown 250 feet, a second was thrown into the air and lodged in a birch tree, while the third was literally blown to pieces, it being necessary to collect the fragments in a sheet. Those killed were: Engineer Harry Belmont, Fireman E. F. Johnson, and Brakeman E. Lamore."[40]

Ralph Peabody remembered it differently: "One day the train was coming down from the upper end with a load of logs. Just as they crossed Spruce Brook Bridge the water ran into the red-hot end of the boiler and the engine blew up, hurling the engineer and fireman into the tree tops, killing them both. The brakeman had got out to set the brakes on the wheels with a long wrench, and so his life was saved."[41]

Court records, in which the only witness, James Cross, testified, placed the accident a short distance above Camp No. 5 and below Camp

Site of the explosion of the Wild River Railroad Engine Shay #1 Near Camp No. 5— 1899
SOURCE OF ORIGINAL PHOTOGRAPH UNKNOWN

No. 9, between Spruce and Red Brooks, not near Camp No. 1, as the newspaper had reported. The crew had been making up a train of loaded log cars, using a Shay engine. On the day of the accident, the engine had made several trips to and from log sidings taking one loaded car at a time down steep tracks to a more level place where it was added to the train. Everything seemed to be progressing normally when suddenly the engine blew up—a horrendous sight for anyone to witness.[42]

In 1900 the United States Census put the population of Hastings at 173.[43] That year Marshall R. Hastings, Major Hastings' eighteen-year-old grandson, became associated with his grandfather and his father, David Robinson Hastings, in the family business in Batchelder's Grant. Meanwhile the unrelated Hastings Lumber Company's cutting operations on the New Hampshire side in Bean's Purchase moved up to the farthest reaches of Wild River Valley, where the lumbermen gazed over the divide on the other side of Perkins Notch into the valley of Wildcat Brook and its mature hemlock, spruce, and fir. There, in 1901, according to Ralph Peabody, the loggers "rigged up a donkey engine and hauled up logs by a wire rope to the top of the slope."[44] From that point, the logs were hauled one to two miles to the Wild River Railroad near Camp No. 9.

During the year 1901 the journalist L. C. Bateman went on a deer-hunting trip into Wild River Valley, staying at Hastings Village and visiting the camps in Batchelder's Grant owned by the Hastings family. He counted "seven separate lumber camps employing one hundred and fifty men and seventy-five horses in steady operation for more than six months in the year." Here, he and the others in his party were hosted by the "genial proprietor of the camp," David R. "Rob" Hastings, who "presented a most picturesque appearance . . . in an old slouch hat, woolen shirt worse for wear, and pant legs and seat in fringes and tatters."[45]

Bateman reported that Mr. Hastings "has a large boarding house where are kept twenty-five of his men who work in his spool and dowel mill close by. In this mill are sawed the spool bars and dowel stock which are shipped to the factories where those articles are finished." He noted that the sawdust from the mill is fed automatically by "a most ingenious device" into the furnace to run the steam engine.[46]

All the development and activity in Wild River Valley at this time, unlike that which would occur in the future, depended on one thing and one thing only—getting the logs out. Bateman discovered that the main or largest lumbering camp that supplied the Hastings family's business was about four miles up a tote road from the village and "is most typical of primitive wood life." He described it as "a large and low structure, built entirely of logs, and chinked up so as to be impervious to wind and storm." At night a visitor might see the loggers "sitting around the room . . . playing cards over the top of a barrel or on a soap box, telling stories, laughing and having what to them is a hilarious good time. . . ."[47]

Bateman recounted that the loggers start out for work at the first break of day, dividing into crews. One crew fells and trims trees. Another, the teamsters, loads the logs into bobsleds, and then, with top ends dragging, hauls the logs to the nearest of five landings on Evans Brook. There, another crew saws the logs into bolts four and five feet long and piles them on the bank of the brook "ready to be tumbled into the water with the first appearance of a spring freshet." This pulp lumber was sold to large companies that manufactured paper downriver on the Androscoggin and was a profitable business for the Hastings enterprise. According to Bateman, the Hastings family owned and managed 22,000 acres of rich forest land, estimated to contain "sixty million feet of pulp lumber, to say nothing of the enormous quantities of hard wood that can be utilized for other purposes."[48]

While the Hastings operation logged Batchelder's Grant, the cutting also continued in Bean's Purchase up into the far reaches of the valley. During this period in the early 1900s, the public was becoming alarmed at the destruction of the country's forests.[49] Concerns were being expressed at the federal level, too, with reports giving a dim assessment of the forests. One noted that little virgin timber was left and went on to say that "throughout the mountains the worse destruction has been on the high slopes and fire has often followed with terrible results. Clear cutting is practiced in all the steeper slopes. The spruce logs are rolled down the slopes to the road below over the merchantable stuff and the hardwoods, which are first felled down the slope and this forms a good rolling bed. The hardwoods are left lying in the ground unused. The result is a veritable fire trap that lasts for years."[50]

These kinds of reports and reactions confirmed the type of logging practiced at the time, and the cutting in Wild River Valley was no different. Not only were the steep slopes denuded, but great piles of slash were left behind. This clear-cutting of the forest was encouraged by the introduction of the railroad and its easy access to timber in the valley and efficient and dependable means of satisfying the insatiable appetites of the mills. The cutting practices were little informed by scientific forestry, which was still in its infancy, and any knowledge of ecological effects was rudimentary. The valley was thus set up for disaster. Indeed, it seemed that the lumbermen were daring one to occur. And it did.

It happened in the spring of 1903. A series of events came together that set in motion the demise of the village of Hastings and Hastings Lumber Company. Sometime in the early months of that year, after loggers had completed their operations along the western boundary of Bean's Purchase just over the Wild River Valley divide, "heavy rain storms . . . washed out much of the railroad and many of the logging roads."[51] This was followed by an unusually dry period, lasting into June. On May 20 concern about the lack of rain began showing up in the *Bethel News*: "A little rain would be very welcome. . . . A heavy fall of rain is much needed. . . . Dust and smoke make the air impure."[52] A few days later, the paper reported: "Farmers are becoming weary watching and praying for rain. . . . The drouth has already become a serious matter; the grass that looked so green and promising three weeks ago has now dried up beyond recovery as the ridges, and all the rest of it will, unless we have some rain soon."[53] The slash and other dead growth on the mountain-sides turned to tinder lacking only a means of ignition to turn the valley into an inferno. One report at the time recognized several possible means of igniting a major fire, including "railroads, carelessness, land clearing, fishermen, campers, and malice."[54] The railroad was a particular threat for Wild River Valley because "the first locomotives burned wood and set out many fires."[55] And of course, beyond human causes, it was well known that lightning in electrical storms also caused many forest fires when dry conditions prevailed.

It was probably inevitable with everything so dry that a forest fire

The ferocity of a forest fire in the White Mountains. This fire in 1908 burned nearly 2,000 acres at the head of Franconia Brook, twenty-two miles from Wild River Valley.
<small>UNITED STATES FOREST SERVICE, WHITE MOUNTAIN NATIONAL FOREST PHOTOGRAPH</small>

would break out in the valley. On June 3 the *Oxford Democrat* reported that "forest fires are being spread by the wind. Smoke, dust, drouth and destruction."[56] *The Mountaineer* wrote that June 3rd "was a 'yellow' day in Gorham. The smoke, as the day advanced, settled thicker and thicker over the village, and when the sun was discernible at all it looked like a big red ball of fire. Ashes fell continually during the day. . . ."[57]

The fire was a pure hell for anything in its path. It roared out of control toward the nearby valley of Wild River, up a mountain slope, and over the top. There, stretched out in the valley below, was a forest fire's delight, an open invitation. Great piles of slash—treetops and limbs—lay in scattered windrows down the steep, clear-cut mountainsides all the way to the river below and up the mountain slopes beyond.[58] A sprinkling of trees, alone and in small stands, dotted the hillsides intermingling with skeletal, windthrown trees, brittle brush, shriveled sprouts, and withered herbs—all dried to fire-prone perfection by fifty days without rain.[59] A deadly triangle had come together: great quantities of ignitable fuel, with much of it loosely arranged like kindling in a fireplace, enough heat from a wildfire to ignite the fuel and sustain continued burning, and a plentiful supply of oxygen from air amply provided and circulated by wind.[60] Wild River Valley was a table set to feed a hungry fire.

With all the ferocity of a starved wolf attacking a running deer, the fire lunged down the slopes with a wind-whipped vengeance, setting upon the tinder with explosive fury. Huge clouds of smoke shot up and burnt debris roiled over the slopes. Searing heat radiated from the slash, brush, and burning trees, creating convection currents that transferred the intense heat to the rocks, soil, and water—everything that it could reach.

Beneath some of the slash piles where the fire burned long enough, temperatures reached more than 900 degrees Fahrenheit, penetrating into the soil deep enough to kill earthworms. The very structure of the land's soil changed in ways that would later increase rain and snow runoff and result in the subsequent loss of soil and nutrients by erosion. The high temperatures destroyed the soil's critically needed organic materials—fragments of partially decomposed plants and animals on the forest floor and in the humus layer. The fire was devastating for living organisms associated with the soil, killing most as temperatures rose to a point at or just below that of boiling water, 212 degrees Fahrenheit. A host of animals did not survive—ants, beetles, mites, centipedes, spiders, grubs, slugs, and snails, to name a few.

On a smaller but extremely critical scale, bacteria and other microorganisms concentrated in the surface litter and upper organic layers of the soil were lost. These organisms are necessary for the decomposition of dead plants and animals and the recycling of nutrients essential to life, such as nitrogen. Other important nutrients affected by the fire included phosphorous and sulfur. Some nutrients were lost into the air when the intense heat vaporized them. Others were blown away as particulates in smoke. The fire also destroyed micorrhizal fungi in the soil's upper layers and the crucial symbiotic relationships they had developed with roots of trees and other plants, helping them obtain nutrients and water over a wide area.[61] Thus, in a short time, the fire reduced to ashes patches of the complex and delicate ecological fabric that had survived the clear-cutting.

Above ground, the fire killed on a much larger, more observable scale. For many animals living in spots skipped by the loggers, the timing of the fire spelled doom because spring is a time for nesting and the raising of young.[62] As it raged down into the valley, its roar would have drowned out the frantic calls and frenzied flapping of birds caught in the approaching inferno. For a number of species, the fire occurred during incubation or the feeding of young. Northern flickers, for example, would have been forced to abandon their eggs in nest trees before they themselves succumbed to the smoke and flames. Even worse, hairy woodpeckers that in all likelihood had bred earlier would have had to leave nest holes containing tiny nestlings.

For ground-nesting birds, death likely came much quicker. Colorful rufous-sided towhees, known to frequent this area, would have just laid eggs for the first of two broods they would raise in concealed, sturdily built nests of leaves and grasses. Chestnut-sided warblers also nested in the same time period on the ground or in low bushes near woodland clearings. So, too, did dark-eyed junco families. Many of the adults probably escaped, leaving their eggs and young behind. In the case of the larger ruffed grouse laying ten or more eggs in shallow nests of leaves in brushy areas, perhaps among clumps of trees left by the loggers, chicks may have had a better chance of survival. The young, able to leave the nest less than a day after hatching, would have scurried after their mothers in a feeble effort to outrun the fire. There is a chance that some escaped by hiding under rocks or logs or perhaps by the flames being diverted around them.

While most of the large adult mammals—moose, deer, bobcats, foxes, and others—would have been able to successfully flee the fire, it is likely that some were too young to get away. For snowshoe hares attracted to the abundance of grasses, ferns, and other succulent plants that had emerged in the clear-cuts before the fire struck, it is likely that more adults escaped than their recently born young, who could not move fast enough to reach protective shelter in time to avoid the heat and flames. Deer mice may have been on their second litter when the fire arrived, but for those nesting deep enough underground, as they are known to do in old chipmunk burrows, the fire would have harmlessly passed over the adults and their nursing young, its lethal temperatures never penetrating deep enough in the ground to affect them. Southern red-backed voles also are known to live in old burrow systems, such as those made by hairy-tailed moles. The moles dig deep tunnel systems in loose, moist soils, and voles lucky enough to have had the safety of such homes were likely unaffected.

The fire swept down between the mountains after entering the headwaters of Wild River, burning the habitat of other animals, such as that of woodland jumping mice near the river. Here, the mice would have been attracted by easy burrowing conditions adjacent to recent clear-cuts offering plentiful supplies of tender plants, seeds, and insects. Although their burrows are often only a few inches deep, large stumps or rocks over some nests might have given enough protection from the heat of the passing fire to allow the small mammals to survive.

The fire spread throughout the upper reaches of the river, where mere trickles of water flowed in drought-dried wetlands and rocky streambeds. Driven by the wind, the fire fanned out, racing up the slopes of the mountains on the other side of the valley. The valley's narrow, V-shaped trough created a Venturi effect, increasing the wind's velocity and pushing the fire down the valley along the river's rock-clogged bed and the tracks of the logging railroad that paralleled it.

As the inferno sped in the direction of Hastings, the villagers watched the billowing smoke in the valley above with growing uneasiness. It's relatively easy to imagine men and women going about their jobs and taking a moment now and then to keep an eye on the upper valley, trying to gauge the fire's advance, and along with their children, worrying about the danger. These were people who lived close to the land and depended on the forest for their livelihood. They would have known all too clearly the threat posed by the prolonged drought and the increasing dry conditions they saw in the valley.

Years later, one resident vividly remembered the fire, saying that "his mother had taken all their belongings out of the house and piled them up where they could be moved quickly. . . ."[63] What she and the others who lived and worked in the valley did not know at the time was that it didn't matter whether or not the fire reached the village; the fire would doom it anyway, and one way or another, they would have to leave.

In the path of the fire halfway down the valley, between its headwaters and the village, the old hemlock stood. For several hundred years, the great tree had witnessed the changes that the valley had undergone. For most of its life, they were rather predictable and orderly changes as nature evolved and matured. To be sure, there were perturbations—dry spells, storms, minor floods, local outbreaks of disease, and insect infestations—but the effects of these eventually, for the most part, had disappeared, and the tree had remained undisturbed. The tree had also survived the advance of the loggers brought into its vicinity by the railroad. But on that June day, the tree faced another threat that could result in its demise.

Small eastern hemlocks are highly sensitive to wildfire, and their shallow root systems can be easily damaged by intense fires. Even a fire of low severity is known to have killed most hemlock saplings in a northern hardwoods community and to have killed or badly damaged 60 percent of its mature trees.[64] Old trees, like the large hemlock, have thicker bark and can withstand light burns. The fire that roared down Wild River Valley that spring day, however, was a large fire. It produced heat never before experienced by the hemlock, nor probably by anything in the history of the valley, for never had there been so much flammable material left lying on the ground over so much of the valley's surface area.

The old tree survived, but it was a close call. A map published two years later shows just how close. The fire stopped short of Blue Brook and probably advanced down the slope of the mountain above the tree before it turned.[65]

A week after the Wild River fire, *The Mountaineer*'s headlines read: "RAIN CHECKS FOREST FIRES. Those in the vicinity of Gorham sub-

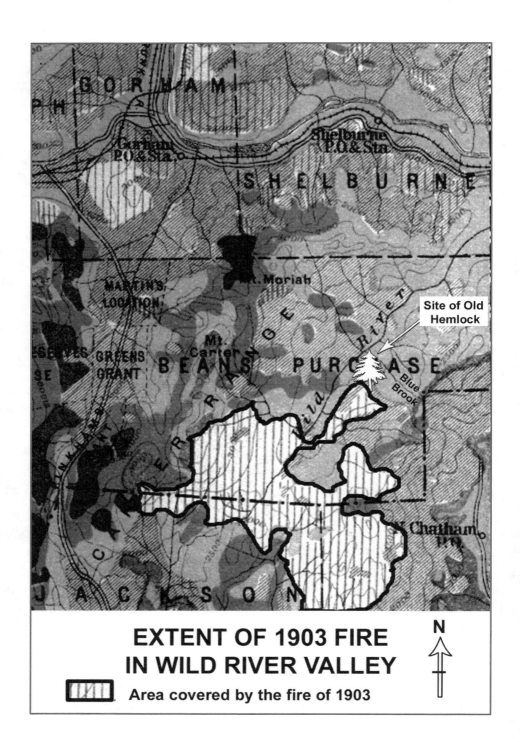

EXTENT OF 1903 FIRE IN WILD RIVER VALLEY

N

Area covered by the fire of 1903

dued. The Damage to Timber Lands in Coos County Estimated at Many Millions—All Fires Now Reported To Be Under Control."[66] For the Hastings Lumber Company, the fire had consumed 12,660 acres of Bean's Purchase in the upper part of Wild River Valley.[67] A report, "Old Burns within the White Mountain Purchase Unit," described it as a "very severe slash fire."[68] All told, approximately 84,250 acres burned in the White Mountain region with a damage estimated at $200,000, although it was mostly cut-over land.[69] The fires of that year, according to observers, "left impressive slow-healing scars."[70] This was true not only for the natural communities of the valley but for the community of Hastings. Between the clear-cutting and the fire, the lifelines of both had been cut—the community's lifeline to its resource base, the forest, and within the forest, the myriad of ecological interconnections that had kept it healthy and alive.

Left: Extent of the 1903 forest fire in Wild River Valley. Reprinted and modified from "Map I. Forest density and land characteristics of northern New Hampshire," in Alfred K. Chittenden, Forest Conditions of Northern New Hampshire, *U.S. Department of Agriculture, Bureau of Forestry, Bulletin 55 (Washington, D.C.: Government Printing Office, 1905), 10.*

PART II

AFTER THE FIRE

Four

Trauma Within

Following the fire, Hastings Lumber Company and village residents, who depended on the timber wealth of Bean's Purchase, found the economic viability of the forest exhausted and in ruin. The railroad had suffered severely, as had some of the lumber camps. The company and village never recovered. The next year, in October 1904, the *Berlin Independent* announced the following under the heading "The Passing of Hastings":

> The recent closing out of lumber operations at Wild River results in the abandonment of the little colony. Last week, Wednesday, saw the last passenger train to run to the settlement. Since Emery Bros. of Portland assumed the ownership, the timber has been rapidly cut off, and now operations are being closed up as fast as possible. The machinery in the mills is being sold and the mills closed . . . with the closing of the mills the settlement has been abandoned.[1]

For the residents of the tiny village working for Hastings Lumber Company, though they could have seen conditions for a viable economy deteriorating, it must have been especially difficult. They had seen their place of work go out of business. They had experienced the trauma of losing their jobs and their homes. They had been forced to face the anxieties of an unknown future, of family uprootedness and instability, of finding a home, securing employment, learning new skills, and meeting new job expectations. Some, however, would continue to find employment, for the settlement was not completely abandoned, as the newspaper article proclaimed.

The vast timberland in Batchelder's Grant in Maine, under ownership and management by the Hastings family, had escaped the fires. In

Aftermath of the Wild River forest fire, 1903
PHOTOGRAPH COURTESY OF THE APPALACHIAN MOUNTAIN CLUB ARCHIVES

the aftermath, the family purchased some of the mills and buildings, as well as machinery and other equipment that were put up for sale by the Hastings Lumber Company. By the end of spring 1905 the family had formed a new corporation, the Hastings Chemical Company, and had acquired all the land and buildings of the village of Hastings, as well as the wood alcohol plant, from Hastings Lumber Company.[2]

It was a good move on the part of the Hastings family. The alcohol mill was overhauled to increase production, and an expert in the business from New York was put in charge. The plant likely made use of jumbo retorts invented in 1897. The original retorts held three-quarters of a cord of wood, but the new ones probably held more. Three thousand cords of wood were soon piled outside the plant. The visiting journalist Bateman, reporting in 1913, said that the plant could make 3,000 gallons of alcohol in one month with a profit of $750.00.[3]

The birch mill and sawmill also did a large business. Pulpwood continued to be driven down Evans Brook and Wild River and sold to the paper companies on the Androscoggin River. The railroad was taken up and the roadbed converted to a roadway for hauling products to the railroad in Gilead. Twice a day a mail team came up the road to the village. The Hastings family business continued to manage the general store, and the school remained open for the children of workers.[4]

A month after the formation of the Hastings Chemical Company in 1905, Major Hastings, in declining health since the death of his wife Dolly the previous year, decided to head west to visit his son Herbert. While there, he died on August 31 at age eighty-four. Wild River Valley and the region lost an influential, respected, and well-known citizen.[5]

The next few years were productive for the Hastings family members as the land in Batchelder's Grant continued to supply the wood on which their business was based. But would it be another temporary economy, an unsustainable prosperity, like that experienced by those who had depended on the forest resource in Bean's Purchase? The result of not maintaining a sustainable forest had been graphically demonstrated right next door following years of public warnings. Well before the disastrous fire of 1903, concern about the health of the forest in Maine and New Hampshire, as well as in other states, had been rising among members of the public.

In Maine at the time the village of Hastings was being built, the state created the Maine Forest Commission and the position of forest commissioner. Although the legislation carried no authorization of funds, it was nevertheless an official response to the public's interest in the forests of the state.[6] In New Hampshire, in the early 1880s when the Hastings family was establishing its business in Batchelder's Grant, a forest conservation initiative was spawned by a public concerned about widespread clear-cutting of the state's forests and its detrimental effects on soil erosion, stream control, fire danger, and tourist visitation. Over the next decade, two separate New Hampshire Forestry Commissions were formed, culminating in the Forestry Law of 1893.[7]

In spring 1893 the New York-based periodical *Garden and Forest* reported on the second New Hampshire Forestry Commission's findings and conclusions. The report was relevant to what was occurring in Wild River Valley at the time:

> Unwise methods of cutting the timber and the degradation of the soil of the forest-floor after the trees have been cut have reduced the capacity of the region, as a whole, to produce timber. In some portions of the White Mountain territory the forest conditions are said to have been permanently ruined. . . . The soil has been burnt out and swept away down to the inner rocks, leaving bare slopes upon which trees can never grow again for lumber or any other use. Over some areas the beauty, attractiveness and value of the unequaled White Mountain scenery . . . has been entirely blotted out, and this extinction of sylvan beauty and of its commercial value is permanent. . . .[8]

The report did result in the New Hampshire Forestry Law of 1893, but this law, like the first Maine law, turned out to be only a small first step.

That same year, the Boston-based Appalachian Mountain Club (AMC) held its annual field meeting in Jefferson, New Hampshire. Much of the agenda dealt with the threat of destructive logging practices in the White Mountains. The organization put its weight of influence on the United States Congress to enact forest protection laws. But it would take years before Congress enacted legislation.[9]

Although the results of these conservation efforts were too late to save Wild River Valley from the fate it suffered, a trend toward better forest management was slowly occurring. The country's first four-year forestry degree program at Cornell University was established in 1898. Three years later a group of citizens concerned about logging practices in northern New Hampshire formed the Society for the Protection of New Hampshire Forests. "Their mission: to protect the White Mountains, which are rapidly being clear-cut."[10] The society grew to have a powerful influence on land conservation and the prevention of the forest resource being lost to development. And at this time, around the turn of the century, the ideas of scientific forestry, sustainable yield, and conservation were beginning to make their entry into the American mind.

In 1903, a time when the beginning of the end of Hastings Village and the conclusion of the long series of events that devastated the primeval natural character of Bean's Purchase were occurring, the New Hampshire State Legislature funded a study to determine, among other things, "the conditions existing in the forest and the causes of those conditions, [and] to estimate the cost and devise the methods necessary to the preservation of the forest of the White Mountain region and ultimately of the whole state. . . ."[11]

The author of the report on the study was Alfred K. Chittenden, assistant forest inspector with the United States Bureau of Forestry. Among the forest areas investigated was the Carter Range. The southern slopes of the range are drained by Wild River, and the report noted that they "have been pretty well cut over. A logging road was run the entire

A once heavily timbered mountain in the White Mountain National Forest after clear-cutting and fire. North Sugarloaf Mountain, eighteen miles west of Wild River Valley, is seen here in 1903 practically barren after being subjected to clear-cutting and fire. Reprinted from Alfred K. Chittenden, Forest Conditions of Northern New Hampshire, *U. S. Department of Agriculture, Bureau of Forestry, Bulletin 55 (Washington, D.C.: Government Printing Office, 1905), 64a.*

length of the valley, and the lower slopes were cut over first for sawlogs only, and now contain an irregular forest of hardwoods, with considerable spruce suitable for pulpwood. The more recent lumbering, as that in the Moriah Brook Valley, has been severe, taking both saw and pulp logs. A scattering of hardwood growth is all that remains, aside from a few small patches of virgin spruce on the upper and more inaccessible slopes. The upper part of Wild River Valley was severely burned in the spring of 1903, and but little growth now remains."[12]

The Chittenden report showed that science at the time could provide an overall assessment of the effects of clear-cutting and fire on forested land. However, it would be a long time before scientific research reached a sophistication that would enable it to identify with increasing precision the ecological variables affected by clear-cutting and quantify them and their effects. In fact, it would be more than a half century later, in the 1960s, before scientists began a long-term ecological study project that seemed particularly suited to explaining what happened to the ecosystems in the old hemlock's once pristine valley.

The study's location was the Hubbard Brook watershed, a little more than one hundred miles southwest of Wild River Valley in the White Mountain National Forest. It began in 1960 with an idea conceived by Dr. F. Herbert Bormann, a botany professor and forest ecologist at Dartmouth College. He saw in small forested watersheds opportunities to "study ecosystem functions and the connection of the ecosystem to the atmosphere and hydrosphere."[13] He proposed this to Dr. Robert S. Pierce of the Hubbard Brook Experimental Forest in the White Mountain National Forest.

The next year, Dr. Gene E. Likens, an aquatic ecologist, took a faculty position at Dartmouth. Bormann and Likens joined forces, invited a geologist to join them, procured funding, and the Hubbard Brook Ecosystem Study was born. Their initial approach was to use "the chemistry of stream water draining out of a watershed like the diagnostic approach a physician uses in measuring the chemistry of blood or urine in a human patient" in order to measure the health of an ecosystem and better understand its basic functions.[14] By 2003, more than forty years later, the study had resulted in more than 1,200 published articles and six books from more than sixty principal researchers and scores of Ph.D. students.

What makes the Hubbard Brook project of interest in explaining the ecological effects of the early timber operations in Wild River Valley is its studies of clear-cutting in a watershed that is, in the words of a publication on the Hubbard Brook website, "characteristic of much of the White Mountain National Forest."[15] This could also be said of Wild River Valley, which, like the watershed of Hubbard Brook, has "hilly, occasional steep topography; coarse, acidic, glacially derived soils; bedrock dominated by metamorphic rock of igneous and sedimentary origin; northern hardwood forests on lower slopes and spruce-fir on upper reaches; and continental climate of long, cold winters and mild to cool summers."[16] It is likely, therefore, that many of the studies of clear-cutting in the Hubbard Brook Experimental Forest will help identify and describe the ecological effects of the clear-cutting in Wild River Valley at a time when its logging railroad was in operation.

Those who did the cutting in Wild River Valley in the late 1800s and early 1900s were certainly aware of the gross effects of clear-cutting on the valley's environment: uncontrolled runoff, erosion, sedimentation, loss of cover for animal life, and other observable changes. As we have seen in Chittenden's report, scientific foresters could identify additional factors and make ecological connections. But as the researchers in the Hubbard Brook Ecosystem Study observed in the latter half of the twentieth century, clear-cutting "causes major changes in the environment. All forms of plant and animal life undergo change. Gross changes are readily seen. What is not seen or readily detected are some of the subtle, gradual, yet perhaps highly significant, changes."[17] And as two researchers who studied clear-cutting noted: "The effects of such alteration reverberate throughout the system."[18] This is because, as we saw in the pristine environment in which the old hemlock grew to maturity, the valley's forest ecosystems are composed of closely interrelated parts—water, land, plants, and animals—that are also affected by weather and climate and by topography, including elevation, slope of the land, and the direction of slope. More precisely, the connections or linkages among the ponds, streams, wetlands, and various land-based, or terrestrial, ecosystems involve the flow of energy and exchange of nutrients that occur because of the movement of air, water, and animals across landscape and ecosystem boundaries.[19] Clear-cutting can disrupt these connections and result in the loss or diminishment of parts of ecosystems.

Because of advancements in science, the unseen story is clearer today when we look back and picture the loggers as they moved up into the valley of Wild River. Trees came down to the ring of double-bitted axes. Limbs fell where they were clipped. Saws rasped. Horses dragged logs over undisturbed soils that had taken thousands of years to develop. Canopies disappeared. Multiple levels of leaves delicately arranged to capture light lay in disarray, withering on the forest floor. No longer, however, would these leaves intercept water from rainstorms and break the rain's fall to the forest floor or facilitate the evaporation and transpiration of moisture. Nor would they be available to withhold water from the soil to create a necessary water deficit that would reduce the chance of flooding in times of excess water. And in places where the boots of men, the hoofs of horses, and the gouging of logs had severely disturbed and packed down the forest's porous soil, water could no longer be prevented from running freely down the slopes, stealing centuries of accumulating sediments and discarding them haphazardly elsewhere.[20]

The clear-cutting we can now picture in Wild River Valley interrupted the buildup of organic matter, or humus, on the forest floor—an upper layer, or horizon, of the soil, typically one to eight inches thick in the White Mountains. It did this by preventing the regular accumulation of litter on the forest floor—branches, twigs, leaves, and other debris from trees—and the growth of plants adapted to life beneath the once sheltering canopy. Without a source of these materials to develop this critical layer of soil, the soil would not be able to maintain nutritional quality, hold moisture, and contribute habitat for important soil microorganisms and other living things on which the forest's diversity and growth depend.[21]

If we could have followed the loggers up into their cutting operations in Wild River Valley at the turn of the twentieth century and looked out over the clear-cut landscape, we would not have seen the full damage. We would not have seen the impaired ability of the valley's mature ecosystems, with their tightly developed nutrient cycles, to maintain what was once only a relatively small loss of nutrients in the river and its tributaries. We would not have observed the lessened effectiveness of ecosystems to conserve such losses by storing nutrients and influencing the flow of water through the soil. Nor would we have been able to perceive the weakened capability of mechanisms to carry on natural recycling functions and nutrient regulation.[22] We would not have readily seen the increased loading of nutrients, such as phosphorous and nitrogen, in the streams because of the clear-cutting, nor would we have easily detected the rising acidity of the drainage waters that would affect the stream's organisms.[23] We would not have known that the loss of nitrate, for example, could have been forty to fifty times higher than before the clear-cutting.[24]

Some scientists in the 1970s, while acknowledging that their studies did not extend long enough for concise conclusions, nevertheless reported that "the evidence clearly shows that clearcutting causes a substantial removal of nutrients from the soils investigated." Such losses, the researchers speculated, may extend for at least three years after the harvesting operations.[25] Other researchers note that nutrient losses vary with local conditions, such as slope, drainage, vegetation, and degree of soil disruption.[26]

A comparison of streamflow before and after the clear-cutting in Wild River Valley would have revealed increased flow following cutting, as well as the deposition of sediment in streams. A loss of shading in some streams, because of the removal of trees and other vegetation, would have been readily seen, but the increase that occurred in stream temperature and its influence on chemical reactions and the metabolism of aquatic plants and animals would not have been so apparent.[27] It would not have been known that two to three years after the clear-cutting, its effects on light, temperature, nutrients, and sediment particles in streams flowing out of clear-cut areas compared to those areas that were uncut could have caused the densities of small organisms, such as mayflies, stoneflies, caddisflies, beetles, and sideswimmers (macroinvertebrates) to increase by two to four times.[28]

Could the clear-cut forest of Wild River Valley have fully recovered from the alteration of its delicate, complex ecological structure and interference with its life processes? We know, for example, that measurements of nutrients, such as nitrate, calcium, and potassium, in stream water flowing out of cut-over experimental watersheds, which showed large net losses, peaked in the second year after cutting but gradually returned to precutting levels at rates unique to each nutrient. Yet decades after the cuts, researchers could still see subtle to large differences in nutrients such as calcium in stream water. Their analyses suggested that a cut done in 1965–66 "was still affecting ecosystem function in 2003."[29] It was also found that "100 years or more are required for organic debris dams in headwater streams to reform following their loss due to disturbance from deforestation.[30]

Another long-term study showed that sixty-four years after clearcutting, where slash remained on the ground, the organic matter and nutrient content in the forest floor had substantially recovered.[31] Data from another study found that organic matter will accumulate to a depth equivalent to that at the time of cutting in somewhat more than sixty-five years.[32] Other data indicate that by a hundred years after heavy forest cutting the northern hardwood forest would be comparable to old-growth forests in number of trees, the area of the forest floor that their trunks cover, and the amount of living matter.[33] It is also acknowledged by scientists, however, that we still have much to learn about the dynamics of fungi, bacteria, and other microorganisms in the control of forest recovery and productivity.[34]

So, we might ask, should clear-cutting be practiced today? Some researchers agree that clear-cutting is an acceptable practice for harvesting timber, but they caution that short- and long-term degradation of the forest ecosystem can occur unless safeguards are exercised, such as limiting clear-cutting to sites with fertile soils on modest slopes while avoiding steep slopes and thin soils; limiting size of clear-cuts to maximize seed regeneration and minimize runoff, nutrient loss, and sediment removal in streams; limiting damage to the forest floor and overuse of roads and skid trails; avoiding stream-channel damage; encouraging early successional plant growth, using 110- to 120-year cutting rotations; and planning to provide for high water quality and protect aquatic ecosystems.[35] It is unlikely that even a few of these precautions were taken during the heyday of Hastings Village before the disaster of 1903.

Others have raised concerns about clear-cutting that reflect values different from its direct, consumptive economic value for wood products. While most of these opponents of clear-cutting recognize the need for logging, they object to clear-cutting as being ecologically indefensible. They believe that clear-cutting causes irreparable damage to the biological diversity upon which life depends. They point out that much damage is too small or subtle to see and may not show up for many years. Some see clear-cuts as a scenic blight on the landscape and aesthetically displeasing. Some argue that moral and spiritual values are destroyed by clear-cutting. Still others take the view that we must protect large areas as wilderness while managing the remainder for multiple use and for mimicking natural processes in management practices. And there are those who believe that sustainable forestry will only be possible if we lower our demand for wood products.[36] In recent years, questions and concerns have been raised about the relationship between clear-cutting and global climate change.

In 2005, only a few miles north of Wild River Valley, the clear-cutting of a 22,500-acre parcel of private land touched off yet another debate about the extent to which clear-cutting allows the forest to sustain itself and continue to produce commercially valuable wood while avoiding ecological collapse. The issue also provoked other worries: the worry over the possibility of liquidation harvesting, in which loggers-turned-landowners cut the land heavily and then sell it off for development of second homes and businesses; and the worry over loss of wildlife habitat and public access for traditional outdoor recreation activities. The article brought home the point that a century after Wild River Valley experienced ecological havoc; people were still debating the pros and cons of clear-cutting.[37]

While we now know more clearly how clear-cutting probably took its toll on the ecological systems in which the old hemlock grew to maturity in Wild River Valley, what of forest fires and their effects? Interestingly, there is very little evidence that forest fires in the northern hardwood forests of the White Mountains during presettlement times were widespread and frequent, leading scientists to believe that, in this case, the value of forest fire as an ecological factor was relatively unimportant. After 1869, however, the large-scale, slash-clear-cutting in the White Mountains, such as that in Wild River Valley, drastically increased forest fires and their effects on ecosystems. In the twentieth century, when fire protection measures were instituted, fire occurrence became relatively rare again.[38] Today, ecological understanding has advanced to a point where fires are prescribed in the White Mountain National Forest in some management areas for wildlife habitat and other benefits.

Two years after Wild River Valley burned, Chittenden reported that "fires on cut-over lands usually kill all standing timber left on areas burned, as well as all the young growth."[39] It was, however, fire's effect on the soil upon which plants depend that Chittenden had much to say. "The importance of the accumulation of organic matter as a constituent of forest soil can hardly be overestimated," he wrote, going on to discuss its value in holding moisture, acting as a fertilizer, and making possible forest growth on steep mountain slopes. He pointed out that it is fire's destruction of this organic matter, or humus, that leads to the loss of nitrogen and other valuable mineral plant foods. A severe fire on steep slopes burns "the intricate network of fine rootlets which constitutes the major part of the humus . . . [and] rain falling on the bare soil quickly carries away in solution not only all the soluble mineral plant food liberated by the fire, but also the finest and most valuable particles of the soil itself. . . . Slopes of this type, owing to the rapidity of the erosion and the slowness with which they become reseeded to forest trees, are usually lost to forest production."[40]

Scientists today would also agree that the immediate effect of the fire likely killed many plants left after the cutting, burned organic material and woody debris in its path, smothered the area in smoke, and created changes in the chemical and physical conditions of its natural ecosystems. Temperatures below 212 degrees Fahrenheit can be fatal to most living organisms. When temperatures reach 428 degrees Fahrenheit, soil loses its water. Between 428 and 860 degrees Fahrenheit, organic matter combusts and can destroy soil structure.[41] Chemically, fire alters nutrient cycling processes by volatilizing nutrients, by affecting decomposition and mineralization—processes that make nutrients available to plants—and by increasing the loss of nutrients through greater runoff and erosion.[42] Other changes that occurred after the fire likely affected microclimate, soil temperature, soil nutrients, microbial activity, succession and regeneration of vegetation, plant growth rates, wildlife habitat and animal activity, water storage capacity, and runoff patterns.[43]

Less than a half century after the fire, the ecologist-philosopher Aldo Leopold was to say: "A prudent technology should alter the natural order as little as possible."[44] There is no question that the natural order in Wild River Valley was greatly altered during the era of the railroad and Hastings Village. The question was: How much of the natural order survived in the valley and could we humans help nurture it back to health?

Five

Nature's Renewal

In the early part of the century after the fire of 1903, Bean's Purchase saw comparatively little timber harvesting, and because the area was left alone, the forest began to grow back. A broad-winged hawk soaring over the valley each summer's breeding season would have seen a blanket of green gradually cover the scarred landscape as plants emerged, sprouted, and grew.

Early successional herbs and shrubs—pin cherry, raspberry, hay-scented fern, and others—pioneered the forest's restoration. Roots of trees crept outward and limbs and twigs grew toward the light-filled openings. Sprouts shot upward from the stumps and roots of beech, striped maple, and other trees. Seedlings sprang up from sprouted seeds that had blown in from nearby trees. As time passed, fast-growing species of trees and shrubs that craved sunlight gained a foothold. These were intolerant-to-shade species, such as white and gray birch and trembling and big-tooth aspen. Some intermediate intolerant species, such as red and striped maple, also grew in the openings. Grasses, broad-leaved herbaceous plants, shrubs, and tree saplings provided a dense cover for the browsing and foraging of mammals, and food and cover for birds and other wildlife. The trees and shrubs produced shade and a more favorable microclimate for fungi and invertebrates living in the soil and dead wood. Deer and moose were attracted to the proliferation of browse. Over the years saplings became trees, spreading a wider and wider canopy. Upright dead trees (called snags) killed by the fire decayed and fell, while others, which had become more decay-resistant by the fire's heat, survived for years. Two decades after the fire, species of trees that could grow in shade, such as beech, balsam fir, and eastern hemlock, began to exert a presence in the competition for dominance in the developing forest. Because of the heavy cutting and the fact that the fire required replacement of entire stands of trees, animal communities were still recovering three decades or more into the twentieth century.[1]

In the meantime, nature's repair of the ecological devastation experienced in Bean's Purchase got the protection it needed for the valley's recovery. On March 1, 1911, President Howard Taft signed into law the Weeks Act, which created a National Forest Reservation Commission and authorized the federal acquisition and protection of lands in the watersheds of navigable streams. The secretary of agriculture was charged with the responsibility of recommending such lands to the commission and purchasing those lands approved by the commission.

On March 27 Forest Service chief Henry G. Graves submitted recommendations for purchase of the land under the new law. While acknowledging the improvement of navigable streams as the act's fundamental purpose, Graves listed other important benefits, including protection of soil from erosion on mountain slopes, protection of the soil's forested cover from fires, preservation of water power by controlling streamflow, preservation of the purity and dependability of water supply, preservation of timber supply for industries, and preservation of the beauty and attractiveness of upland for the recreation and pleasure of the people. Graves singled out the Appalachian Mountains and White Mountains in the East for priority, citing their special need for protection under the law because of their altitude and steepness and their lack of protection as sources of navigable streams.

Among areas within the White Mountains in New Hampshire and Maine that Graves specifically invited proposals from landowners to sell were Bean's Purchase and Batchelder's Grant.[2] Three years later, on March 30, 1914, Bean's Purchase was sold by the Hastings Lumber Company to the federal government.[3] Henceforth, the New Hampshire portion of Wild River Valley would be managed for multiple values, not just for the economic value of its timber for manufactured wood products.

While Bean's Purchase was experiencing a major change that would affect its future management, the Hastings family business— Hastings Chemical Company—continued to harvest its holdings in Batchelder's Grant. In 1913 the company "put 7,000 cords of pulp on the river and had

2,000,000 feet of hard wood sawed."[4] The cutting eventually took its toll, and two years later, a forest examiner surveyed the land in the grant and found that "the tract was cutover for softwoods, both pulp and sawtimber, and some of the best hardwood old growth and paper birch had been removed. . . ."[5]

In 1918 the Hastings enterprise sold its land in Batchelder's Grant, with the exception of the site of Hastings Village, to the federal government to become part of the White Mountain National Forest. A little more than a decade later, on February 25, 1929, the Hastings family sold the village site to the federal government.[6] The whole valley now came under a radically different approach to management than that of the previous century. Instead of cut-and-move-on timber harvesting for immediate economic gain, the new manager, the United States Forest Service, took a longer view for managing the forest resource. This new guiding philosophy had been introduced earlier by Forest Service chief Henry S. Graves, who said that management would be concerned with securing "the maintenance of a perpetual growth of forest."[7]

Grave's predecessor was Gifford Pinchot, the first chief of the Forest Service. He served under President Theodore Roosevelt from 1905 to 1910. Pinchot guided the organization toward the philosophy of managing the forest resource for the "greatest good for the greatest number," adding the phrase "in the long run." He was very critical of the cutting practices of the past, and had once written that "when the Gay Nineties began, the common word for our forests was 'inexhaustible.' To waste timber was a virtue and not a crime. There would always be plenty of timber. . . . The lumberman . . . regarded forest devastation as normal and second growth as a delusion for fools. . . ."[8]

Pinchot and Graves set the direction of management by the Forest Service for Wild River Valley and its natural ecosystems and resources, especially toward the goal of a sustainable yield of timber. Before the end of the century, the Forest Service's philosophy would broaden and reflect a widespread concern for landscape character. Indeed, how to care for the forest's natural landscape character would be identified as a management problem to be taken seriously, along with providing for recreational experiences.[9] Multiple use of the forest and a sustained yield of products and services for long-term public benefit and a sound environment were the goals.[10]

In 1916, two years after the sale of Bean's Purchase to the United States government, a Forest Service forester evaluated an area south of Wild River extending westward from the Maine–New Hampshire line for a potential timber sale. The tract under consideration came close to the area where the old hemlock was standing. The forester inspected the parcel in response to an application by the Sullivan Chemical Company to purchase and cut 10,000 cords of hardwood pulpwood followed by annual harvesting of 5,000 cords. The company planned to convert the wood into distillation products—charcoal, acetate of lime, and wood alcohol. This would be done at "the old distillation plant" located in the opening at Hastings, Maine. The company, it turned out, had leased the plant from Hastings Chemical Company.[11]

The report prepared by the forester illustrated the stark difference between the forest management view advocated by the Forest Service and the 1890s view. Instead of cut-and-run for the greatest profit, the Forest Service was guided "not only from a financial point of view, but also from a silvicultural point of view that considered such factors as erosion susceptibility and condition of trees."[12] The sale was made, and the Sullivan Chemical Company operated the plant for about two years, ceasing operation when it was determined that the business was unprofitable.[13] Just why the plant failed is not clear, but the area had been heavily cut over only twenty years before, and the trees were relatively small for a good source of wood.

One of the first developments in the valley for a use of the land that was unconnected to the harvesting of trees for wood products occurred in 1922. Five years earlier the State of New Hampshire had passed a law providing for the creation of wildlife refuges with consent of landowners. It was a time when the scarcity of wildlife was a concern, and the concept of wildlife conservation was relatively new. The state's Fish and Game Commission, learning of the success of efforts to increase wildlife populations in sanctuaries elsewhere, embarked on a plan in the 1920s to provide sanctuaries in selected locations. These were enthusiastically embraced by the state during the 1920s and 1930s.[14]

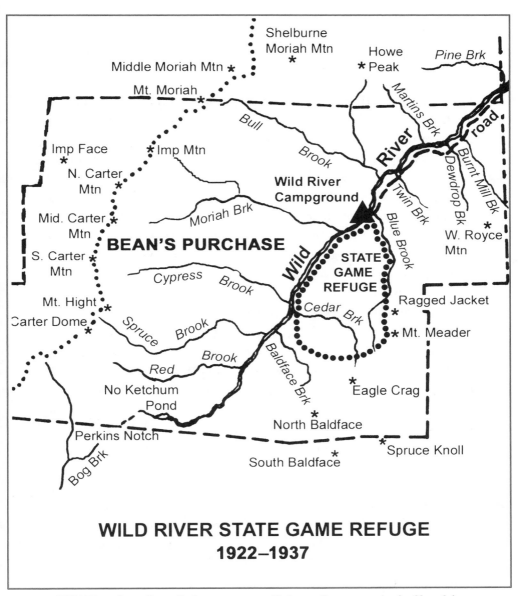

WILD RIVER STATE GAME REFUGE
1922–1937

Wild River State Game Refuge — 1922–37. Redrawn from a copy in the files of the United States Forest Service, White Mountain National Forest, Androscoggin Ranger District.

In 1922 the National Forest Reservation Commission, working with the Forest Service, created the Wild River State Game Refuge in Bean's Purchase. The 3,140-acre refuge extended southward from the confluence of Blue Brook and Wild River, its eastern boundary following two miles along Blue Brook to the top of Mt. Meader, and its western boundary following Wild River for nearly three miles. The southern boundary of the refuge stopped just short of Eagle Crag. The country within the refuge was mountainous and contained Cedar Brook, several smaller streams, and at its northern end, the old hemlock.

There is evidence that a fence encircled the refuge, and it is speculated that it was a mesh fence, called page wire fencing, with rectangular openings designed to keep wildlife inside.[15] This is a common kind of farm fencing. The height of the fence is uncertain, but it is likely that posts were from twelve to sixteen feet apart, as is usually the case in constructing this fence. The refuge existed until 1937, when it appears to have been abandoned, possibly because of waning interest on the part of the state or Forest Service.[16]

By the time the game refuge was established in Bean's Purchase, the forest had begun to mature. Shorter-lived, faster-growing intolerant trees were shifting to longer-lived, slower-growing tolerant trees such as beech, balsam fir, sugar maple, and eastern hemlock. The growth of understory plants and other trees increasingly controlled the loss of water and nutrients from the forest soils. The woods were making a comeback.[17]

In 1926, before its sale to the United States government, the Hastings Village parcel was also being reclaimed by nature. At that time, perhaps only five or six structures remained. There were two small cultivated fields in the west corner of the parcel and a large expanse of grazing field between Evans Brook and the north side of the road paralleling it, and somewhat less on the south side. This road was gravel, as was another road passing through the former center of the village up along the river. Other more primitive woods roads and numerous footpaths crossed the parcel. A culled patch of woodland, from which the best trees had been selected, had been left just west of the center of the area. Large areas of spruce and hardwood second growth covered the southwestern half of

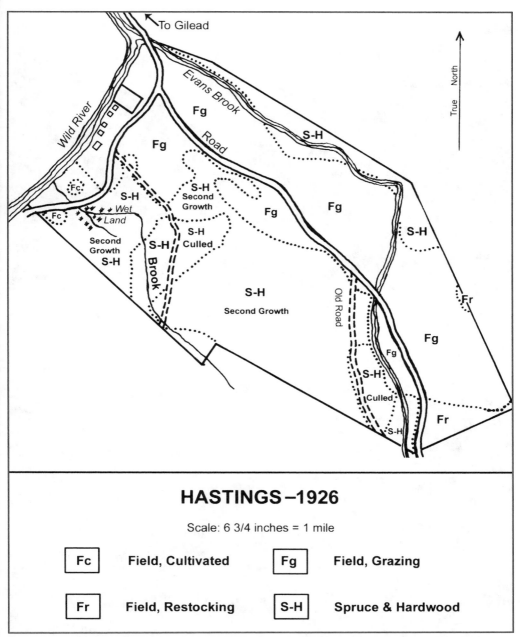

HASTINGS – 1926

Scale: 6 3/4 inches = 1 mile

Fc	Field, Cultivated		**Fg**	Field, Grazing
Fr	Field, Restocking		**S-H**	Spruce & Hardwood

Hastings — 1926. Redrawn from a copy in the files of the United States Forest Service, White Mountain National Forest, Androscoggin Ranger District.

Above: Wild River Valley from The Roost — 1930s
Below: Evans Notch and Speckled Mountain from The Roost — 1930s
BOTH PHOTOGRAPHS COURTESY OF THE UNITED STATES FOREST SERVICE,
WHITE MOUNTAIN NATIONAL FOREST

the land. A clearing still remained, but the woods were rapidly encroaching on it.[18]

In the 1930s a new community appeared at the site of the old village of Hastings—an encampment of young men employed in a new federal program called the Civilian Conservation Corps. Its goals were just the opposite of those behind the establishment of Hastings. The program would have a profound effect on the valley, particularly because of the roadway the Corps would build.

The Civilian Conservation Corps began with a crash—the stock market crash of 1929. Speculative and reckless investing had driven up stocks almost 700 percent during the 1920s.[19] Then panic had set in, and investors began selling their stocks as they lost confidence in the stability of the market and its future growth. In the following days, the market plunged. The Dow Industrial Average dropped from 400 to 145, losing

Site of Hastings Village looking east toward The Roost — 1930s

over $5 billion in the value of stock shares. Millionaires went bankrupt, and many committed suicide. Banks failed, 10,000 of them, because of their lost investments in the stock market. Depositors lost as much as $140 billion.[20] The Great Depression followed the stock market crash. Widespread poverty stalked the land. By the beginning of the 1930s, 4,340,000 were unemployed. Millions were without savings. Businesses closed their doors and communities could not collect taxes to pay for government expenses.[21]

In the fall of 1932 the nation's citizens, shaken and insecure from the collapse of the economic system and its traumatic consequences, went to the polls with change in mind. In a decisive election, they voted in Franklin D. Roosevelt, who had promised that as president he would support a "New Deal." Roosevelt was especially concerned about the lack of jobs and the need to put Americans back to work making a living. Among the measures Roosevelt initiated under his "New Deal" was the Civilian Conservation Corps, or CCC, as it became popularly known. The measure was passed by Congress on March 31, 1933. It gave Roosevelt the authority to enlist thousands of unemployed young men in the work of conserving of the nation's natural resources. And it would

Muster, Civilian Conservation Corps, Wild River Camp, Maine, 156th Company — 1930s
CIVILIAN CONSERVATION CORPS PHOTOGRAPH

lead to the development of another community in that clearing once known as Hastings Village.

Events moved quickly. On April 5 President Roosevelt, by executive order, approved Robert E. Fechner as national conservation director. Roosevelt selected four federal agencies to administer the program, including the Department of Agriculture and its Forest Service, which would ultimately administer a CCC camp in Wild River Valley, and he approved funding.[22] The CCC became known as Roosevelt's Tree Army because of its focus on tree planting. In the life of the Corps (1933–42), 3 billion trees were planted by enrollees. This wasn't the only work the Corps performed. Approximately 300 different kinds of projects were defined for CCC work, including bridges, fire towers, woods telephone lines, truck roads, erosion controls, flood prevention, timber stand improvement, forest protection, recreational development, wildlife habitat improvement, and surveying. Eventually, over 3 million people received employment and stayed in 4,500 camps across the country.[23]

Recruiting for the program began as soon as possible. Enrollees had

Camp work, Civilian Conservation Corps, Wild River Camp, Maine— 1930s
CIVILIAN CONSERVATION CORPS PHOTOGRAPH

to be male, between ages eighteen and twenty-five, physically fit, unemployed, and unmarried. They signed up for six months. Later, the age range for eligibility was changed to seventeen to twenty-eight years and service time was incresaed up to two years. Each accepted enrollee received payment of $30.00 per month, but $25.00 had to be sent home to his family. Maine had an allotment quota of 1,500 youth divided among the state's sixteen counties. Recruiting centers were established in Bangor and Portland, and new recruitments were sent to induction centers at Fort Williams and Fort Preble military posts for conditioning, orientation, and assignment to companies prior to traveling to work camps.[24]

By June 30, 1933, fourteen CCC camps in Maine were open. Nationwide, 250,000 were enrolled by that date. One of the camps in Maine was the Wild River Camp, under supervision of the U.S. Forest Service. It was located at the former site of Hastings Village.[25] The camp opened on May 30 with two hundred recruits in the 156th Company. Tents had been set up earlier by an army unit, and moveable, eight-man buildings had been provided for staff members experienced in forestry and related technical matters. They had been recruited by the Forest Service to work with the CCC boys, as they were called. A superintendent and his wife had moved into a former camp, the only building still standing from the old village complex. Little evidence of the old community of Hastings remained except for foundations. By that time, most of the rails of the logging railroad had been removed from the valley. Work was begun on more permanent facilities, and by late fall, the CCC camp had several large army-style barracks, a mess hall, recreation hall, camp hospital, administration building, officers' quarters, and a garage.[26]

During the years from 1933 until the camp closed in 1937, the young men in the company engaged in many activities. They built fire lines around the camp, constructed twenty-five miles of trails, maintained miles of additional trails, and carried out flood control and cleanup projects along Wild River. In the summer of 1934 one of the enrollees rescued two people from drowning in the river. Another rescue involved a deer that had a broken leg and became stranded in three feet of snow.[27]

The main project of the company, however, was the Evans Notch Road. The company built seven miles of the eleven-mile road. Today, the road is remembered as one of the special accomplishments of the CCC in Maine.[28] It was a joint project of Company 156 at Wild River Camp at the north end of the road and Company 152 stationed at the Cold River Camp at the south end. The two companies started construction at each end of the road and worked toward each other. The Wild River Company was responsible for constructing the road to the "height of land." It was hard labor for the men who used mostly hand tools— wheelbarrows, shovels, and pickaxes—unlike road building today, which relies on heavy mechanized equipment. Ledges and large tree trunks were dynamited, and bridges were built. By late fall the eleven-mile distance had been brushed out.[29]

The road was completed and officially dedicated on September 14, 1936. At one of the most popular scenic overlooks on the road, the national director, Robert E. Fechner, gave the dedication remarks:

On behalf of our Federal Government and in honor of those who had a part in the work, I take pleasure in dedicating Evans Notch Road to the service of our Nation and to the pleasure of all who may be so fortunate as to visit this beautiful spot in our Nation. I am sure

Constructing Evans Notch Road, Civilian Conservation Corps,
Wild River Camp, Maine — 1930s
CIVILIAN CONSERVATION CORPS PHOTOGRAPH

it will stand as an enduring tribute to one of the finest activities in which our Government has ever engaged.[30]

The road would become Route 113, connecting the heavily used Route 2 at Gilead, Maine, with Route 302 at Fryeburg, Maine, and cutting off nearly sixty miles of driving between the two points. Route 302 would become a well-traveled road from Maine's largest city, Portland, to the White Mountains, and one day it would link up with Interstate 95. Thus, untold numbers of people would use these roads to visit the attractions of the New Hampshire and Western Maine mountains, and the Evans Notch Road would join the Grand Trunk Railway among those developments having the greatest influence on the use of Wild River Valley. The road would draw throngs of visitors to enjoy spectacular views of the mountains and outdoor recreational opportunities—uses that would be reinforced as management of the area increasingly changed to multiple use.

In 1937 the CCC camp at Wild River closed, its major work done with the construction of the Evans Notch Road. Meanwhile, the recovering forest had begun reaching merchantable size, and the Forest Service initiated cruising and inspection activities in preparation for stumpage sales. A considerable amount of this work was done in logging compartments that surrounded and included the area of Blue Brook. In the 1940s, 811 acres of profitable hardwood and spruce were cut in a compartment northeast of Blue Brook around Dew Drop Brook, about seven miles from Gilead. A note on the timber sale map indicated that the cutting was to release spruce reproduction.[31]

In September 1947 cruising was completed and a timber sales map was drawn up for harvesting three logging units—Blue Brook, Spider Camp, and Cedar Brook. The mapped area extended four miles along Wild River and two and one-half miles west of the river.[32] The land to be cut included the area where the old hemlock lived, as well as some land burned in the fire of 1903. A sale was made to the Nadeau Lumber Company of Berlin, New Hampshire, and a map for the timber sale was produced and labeled "Part of Wild River Sale—Nadeau—1950."[33] By 1952, approximately 2,500 acres had been harvested. The old hemlock

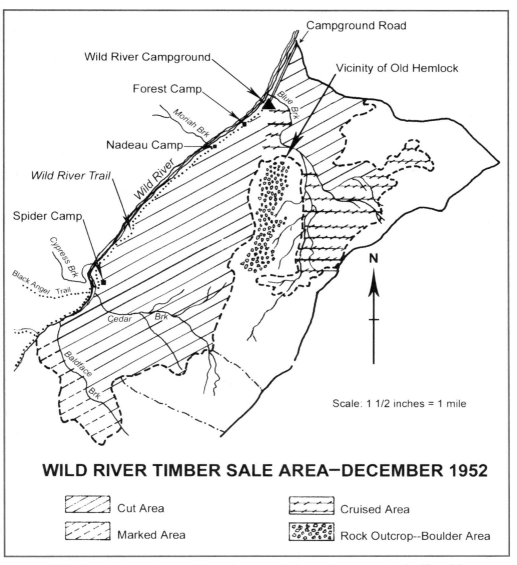

Campground Road

Wild River Campground

Vicinity of Old Hemlock

Forest Camp

Moriah Brk

Blue Brk

Nadeau Camp

Wild River Trail

Wild River

Spider Camp

Cypress Brk

Black Angel Trail

N

Cedar Brk

Baldface Brk

Scale: 1 1/2 inches = 1 mile

WILD RIVER TIMBER SALE AREA—DECEMBER 1952

Cut Area

Cruised Area

Marked Area

Rock Outcrop--Boulder Area

Wild River timber sale area—December 1952. Redrawn from a copy in the files of the United States Forest Service, White Mountain National Forest, Androscoggin Ranger District.

escaped the cutting, possibly because terrain conditions could have made its location difficult to access. The 1947 map shows a large area of rock outcrops and boulders that extends up to the Nadeau cut around Blue Brook and the vicinity of the old hemlock.

Between 1959 and 1990, the Forest Service sold cutting rights on twenty-six parcels, an area nearly 9,000 acres in size. The largest parcel was 2,000 acres on Bull Brook, which was sold in 1959. The smallest parcels were two patches of one acre each. About half of the parcels involved thinning. All but the Bull Brook operation were toward the northeast end of the valley, away from the old hemlock's location. Eighteen of the sales were in Batchelder's Grant on the Maine side of the state line.[34]

With the increasing activity in the woods as surveyors laid out compartment boundaries, cruisers assessed the kind and amount of merchantable timber, and foresters inspected various parcels, it seemed inevitable that the old hemlock would have been found. Yet these activities conducted by the Forest Service resulted in no discovery relating to an old tree's existence. There was, however, another view of the renewing forest beginning to exert itself in Wild River Valley, making it more likely that the old hemlock would be discovered, and it would grow to compete with the entrenched idea that the best use of trees was for manufactured wood products.

Six

DIFFERENT VIEW

Following World War II the valley took on a more natural appearance, looking to some like a wilderness despite the selective harvesting of several parcels. More and more people began coming to the valley for such activities as hiking, camping, canoeing, fishing, and wildlife watching. The increasing numbers reflected a nationwide trend in the recreational use of national forests, parks, and other outdoor areas.

There were many reasons for the public's growing interest in outdoor recreation. The pressures of urban living, with its competitive, impersonal, and stressful atmosphere and its problems of congestion, noise, and pollution, among other assaults on the mind and body, encouraged people to seek respite. Those who sought out the valley and other natural areas looked to satisfy a need for peace of mind, a feeling of harmony, solitude, privacy, aesthetic stimulation, inspiration, and even a spiritual connection with nature—in short, to rejuvenate themselves mentally and physically. Many hoped to gain self-esteem, a feeling of uniqueness, a sense of wholeness, a belief in their own purposefulness and meaningfulness in life, and a clearer perception of reality. They looked for the exhilaration of peak experiences and of overcoming challenges and adversity. They searched for satisfying interpersonal relationships and companionship and wanted to experience the satisfactions of bonding, the sense of belonging, and cooperation with others.[1]

Meeting these needs in the aftermath of the Second World War was made possible by a rising prosperity in the nation; increased leisure time contributed to by shorter workweeks, paid vacations, and holidays; improvements in roads and vehicles; better outdoor gear and recreational equipment; and the availability of maps, guidebooks, and other materials providing directions and descriptions of outdoor areas and information on their use. Among the many destinations popular with the public were the national forests.

Those who visited the White Mountain National Forest and discovered Wild River Valley were provided easy access by the Evans Notch Road and the five-mile road constructed on the old railroad bed up along Wild River. Campgrounds were developed adjacent to the Evans Notch Road near the former site of Hastings Village and at the end of the road up Wild River near the mouth of Blue Brook. For backpacking campers, shelters were built along trails near the summit of Caribou Mountain, along Spruce Brook and, Blue Brook, and at Perkins Notch near No Ketchum Pond. Records show that a trail system in the valley goes back into the 1800s. In 1937 the Appalachian Trail was completed, offering hikers another way into the valley via the west ridgeline. Thus, at the time of the public's rising participation in outdoor recreational activities, Wild River Valley had much to offer visitors, many of whom would retrace the steps of the geologists and early sojourners of the 1800s.

Many visitors were attracted to the river, which in the summer was usually low and flowed gently, looking from a distance like a cobbled street. Here vacationers found pools for fishing and swimming and low ledges for sunbathing. In the lower, less rocky parts of the river, they found opportunities for canoeing. Along major tributaries branching off from the river, trails led hikers up into small side valleys by waterfalls, gorges, and deep ravines, and on up to the high ridges and mountains that surround the watershed of the river, where they enjoyed spectacular views. Visitors were able to backpack for days on the trails from Speckled and Caribou Mountains in the Evans Brook drainage on the Maine side of the valley to the network of trails in and around the main valley of Wild River on the New Hampshire side all the way to the most remote part of the valley in the headwaters of the river around No Ketchum Pond.

Along the trails, hikers were able to take pleasure from their encounters with large old trees, which, like the old hemlock, suggested the natural character of the valley at an earlier time. These old trees were usually seen along mountain trails where steep terrain kept the loggers at bay. The trails also led hikers by small wetlands, beaver ponds, patches of deep woods, and other habitats that produced many chance sightings

Above: Perkins Notch shelter. Nestled deep in the headwaters of Wild River near No Ketchum Pond, this shelter offers respite for the hiker. Carter Dome dominates the background.
Below: Footbridge over Wild River. The height of this footbridge over the river demonstrates how much the river can swell in times of high water and how difficult it was to maintain dams and bridges. BOTH PHOTOGRAPHS BY DEAN B. BENNETT

*The renewal of Wild River Valley's forest is experienced
by a hiker on the High Water Trail*
PHOTOGRAPH BY DEAN B. BENNETT

of wildlife in its natural surroundings.

Through the years the valley, like natural areas all across the country, gained a following. People not only developed a love for the valley but experienced a deeper connection with nature. Over time, they reflected a changing priority of values, tending toward nonconsumptive use of the valley, including wildlife watching, hiking, swimming, and

Moriah Gorge
PHOTOGRAPH BY DEAN B. BENNETT

skiing, vs. consumptive, utilitarian values and uses such as timber harvesting, hunting, and trapping. It was not uncommon for visitors to
return again and again, as did Douglas Schwarz, who camped for many
years with his family at Wild River Campground. His story is like that
of many who discovered the valley and its special attributes.

One of the valley's intriguing natural features that attracted Schwarz was Moriah Brook Gorge with its wild beauty and mystery. Located two and a half miles across the river from the old hemlock, the gorge, like the old tree, had endured the valley's clear-cutting, intrusion of the railroad, and threat of fire, and had survived relatively unscathed. Schwarz, like others had who explored the gorge before him, found its beauty ever more enchanting as he penetrated its depths. The ledges over which the brook flowed appeared, themselves, to flow and to have become molded to the contours of the sparkling effusion of water cascading into the gorge, the product of thousands of years during which the rocks were slowly abraded particle by particle. Where thinly layered intrusions of light-colored quartz and feldspar intersected the darker granites, he discovered that the stream's contouring and polishing had fashioned pleasing patterns, remindful of laminated, wood-turned bowls found in gift stores.

Like so many others who had visited the gorge, Schwarz came away with a haunting impression, unable to fully solve its mysteries because of its dead ends and inaccessible places. Having been unsuccessful in completely exploring the gorge, Schwarz experienced an unfulfilled urge to know what really lay in its depths. Undaunted, he set out one year to learn the gorge's secrets. Equipped to swim and wade, he explored the length of the gorge, but a strange thing happened. When he finally knew its secrets, he said, "I will not describe all that I found in the heart of Moriah Gorge. To do so seems like a violation of a place that should, by rights, remain private." The thing he experienced, he said, made him feel "very small, yet strangely privileged to be part of a large and grander whole."[2] It is not surprising that one day Schwartz would be one who would help throw a lifeline to nature in Wild River Valley.

While the valley's natural character had an influence on the love of nature experienced by those who came to know it intimately, it could influence feelings toward nature in other ways. For example, it was inevitable that visitors would come across physical signs of human attitudes and values toward nature that existed more than a century ago. The signs were in the form of cultural artifacts from the era of Hastings and the Wild River Railroad, when the land was stripped of its forest, the river silted and pushed beyond its banks, the soils robbed of their nutri-

Arthur "Joe" Taylor and Lyle Wiggin on a tour of the ghost town Hastings Village. Remnants of past human use suggest changes in values that have occurred toward Wild River Valley, which now contains thousands of acres of designated federal wilderness.
PHOTOGRAPH BY DEAN B. BENNETT

ents and stability, and the valley left charred, blackened, and devoid of some of its life-forms. These were the artifacts of the late 1800s—crumbling foundations, rusting rails, decaying railroad ties, eroding railroad beds, disappearing logging-camp refuse, gullying of clear-cut slopes, and disintegrating ash and charcoal from the fires—and remnants from the Civilian Conservation Corps' presence in the 1930s and the program's efforts at reforestation, stabilization of river banks, soil and water conservation, and other projects.

The largest collection of artifacts in any one area was, of course, at the old village site of Hastings. For those who were fortunate enough to have had the opportunity to tour the site with Lyle Wiggin and Arthur

Lyle Wiggin, retiree of the United States Forest Service, near the site
of the long-gone sawmill of Wild River Lumber Company
PHOTOGRAPH BY DEAN B. BENNETT

"Joe" Taylor, the experience was enlightening. Both of these men know the old village like their hometowns, for they had worked many years in the valley for the Forest Service. Visitors who followed them through the woods and thickets saw the ruins of one structure after another, and as they did so, the abandoned town grew in both size and complexity. Foundations and other evidence of buildings gone for scores of years were revealed to them. They discovered the locations of railroad spurs that ran to mills near the village. They saw the granite foundation of a sawmill, the lichen-covered stone supports for the saw carriage poking up through vegetation, and piles of bricks where the furnace and stack were located. Beyond, on Evans Brook, they encountered the dry bed of a millpond and a submerged, decayed section of the dam that created it. Deeper into the woods, mounds of old firebricks on the forest floor showed them where another mill once stood. Some distance away, a foundation with some of its plumbing pipes defined to them the location of a boardinghouse. Farther up Evans Brook, they discovered amidst a confusion of plant growth yet another mill and the dam of its millpond. Circling back around to the center of the village near the river, they identified the locations of houses, shops, sheds, and other buildings. It was a fascinating tour, and it left visitors wanting to know more about the history of the village and its effect on the valley.

Farther up the valley, visitors saw other evidence of human use. Those who hiked the Shelburne Trail soon encountered the old bed of the Bull Brook spur of the Wild River Railroad that once followed the brook more than two miles up into the valley. At one time, locomotives hauling logging cars had chugged and clattered past the Bull Brook Logging Camp located about a mile up from the river. This was where the fire of 1895 had swept through thousands of acres, burning slash left from previous cutting.

Hikers who walked the main line of the old railroad bed up the remote, well-wooded valley of Wild River itself also found it difficult to imagine that the woods were once felled and cleared away there, that railroad ties and tracks once lay along the path, that smoke from a fire-ravaged cutting and wood-burning engines once hung in the air. Yet those who were keen, probing observers saw evidence of the valley's history—discarded sections of rail; mounds of displaced earth; a rusting horse-drawn scoop; old bridge timbers; rusted pins in ledges anchoring bridge abutments; old decayed stumps several feet in diameter; pieces of old stoves; broken and rusted parts of engines and railroad cars from accidents, such as the terrible one that occurred near Camp No. 5; and under the forest litter or along the eroded banks of the river, charcoal and ashes from the fire of 1903. Those who happened to stumble onto a site of one of the old logging camps also might have found moss-covered firebricks, piles of old stove parts, snow-shovel blades, crosscut saw blades,

*Arthur "Joe" Taylor examines an engine part discovered
at the site of the 1899 railroad explosion*
PHOTOGRAPH BY DEAN B. BENNETT

chunks of ash, and hand-dug pits of outhouses—all giving a sense of history. Beyond Perkins Notch, explorers who looked closely could have found the site of the donkey engine, lengths of rusting cable, and a ditch made by pulling logs up the steep slope to the horse-drawn sleds that took the logs down to the railroad.

Evidence of a human presence in a landscape that nature has been allowed to reclaim affects people differently. For many, the challenge is to try to reconstruct what the area might once have looked like. Others ask themselves why and how such a landscape was used and, in some cases in Wild River Valley, abused. Some, especially those familiar with history, look at artifacts in a cultural context. For example, historians who learned about Wild River Valley would know that the clear-cutting occurred at a time when it was thought that natural resources were inex-

*Arthur "Joe" Taylor near Perkins Notch examines a
cable for hauling logs up a steep slope*
PHOTOGRAPH BY DEAN B. BENNETT

haustible—one could simply move on after the land in a place had been
plundered and its waters fouled. It was a time when the population of
humans was smaller and people had far less technological ability to affect
the health and sustainability of the land. A few who found evidence of
previous use in an area that was by all appearances wild asked themselves
what kind of ethical relationship with nature is suggested and what it
should be today. [3]

All of this is to say that in the latter half of the twentieth century,
there were likely a few visitors to Wild River Valley who asked questions
about their responsibility toward their natural environment. They would
have been those motivated by a sense of obligation to preserve, in the

Wild River Valley from the Kenduskeag Trail, looking southwest
PHOTOGRAPH BY DEAN B. BENNETT

words of Aldo Leopold, the "integrity, stability, and beauty of the biotic community."[4] They would have been those who wished to see the valley that they had come to love protected. They would have wanted to be able to return year after year and be assured that it was relatively unchanged except by nature. They would have wished to see it preserved as wilderness in perpetuity. Such a dream would become possible in the mid-1960s, for others had begun pursuing the idea on a national scale at the very time Wild River Valley was coming under federal ownership and management.

Aldo Leopold, one of our nation's most eloquent spokespersons for wilderness, had raised the idea as far back as 1921, when he was in the Forest Service. Writing in the *Journal of Forestry*, he wondered "whether the principle of the highest use [of our forests] does not itself demand that representative portions of some forests be preserved as wilderness."[5] His thoughts and words would resonate throughout the growth of the wilderness movement that evolved in concert with the regrowth of nature in Wild River Valley.

From the 1930s into the 1960s, ideas of wilderness preservation took shape in the minds of Leopold and others. The culmination of their persistent and dedicated efforts occurred on September 3, 1964, when the nation officially embraced the value of wilderness with the signing of the Wilderness Act by President Lyndon B. Johnson. The act defined wilderness as follows:

> A wilderness in contrast with those areas where man and his own works dominate the landscape, is hereby recognized as an area where the earth and its community of life are untrammeled by man, where man himself is a visitor who does not remain. An area of wilderness is further defined to mean in this Act an area of undeveloped Federal land [including national forests] retaining its primeval character and influence, without permanent improvements or human habitation, which is protected and managed so as to preserve its natural conditions and which (1) generally appears to have been affected primarily by the forces of nature, with the imprint of man's work substantially unnoticeable; (2) has outstanding opportunities for solitude or a primitive and unconfined type of recreation; (3) has at least five thousand acres of land or is of sufficient size as to make practicable its preservation and use in an unimpaired condition; and (4) may also contain ecological, geological, or other features of scientific, educational, scenic, or historical value.[6]

A key word that would lead to misunderstanding and unintentional or intentional interpretation was the term "untrammeled" in the first sentence of the definition of wilderness. Efforts to preserve wilderness throughout the nation were seriously hampered for years because of this. Untrammeled means unhindered, unrestrained, or allowed free action. Thus, in the definition, "the earth and its community of life" are to evolve freely and naturally, protected from human influence and allowing people only as visitors. To many, the word was understood or interpreted as "untrampled," its root, "trampled," meaning to tread heavily, roughly, or crushingly, to domineer over. Therefore, opponents of the Wilderness Act took the position that any land that had evidence of human use—land that had been "trampled" by humans—was ineligible for wilderness designation. Proponents, on the other hand, interpreted untrammeled as applying to wilderness-designated land that was to be left to evolve and change by natural processes free from human influence. Thus, land that had a past history of human use could qualify for preservation, be protected, and be allowed to return to a natural, wild state.[7]

Following passage of the act, the years during the remainder of the century and beyond were challenging ones for conservationists who tried to protect Wild River Valley and areas all across the nation as wilderness (see Afterword). One of the most difficult obstacles among the many that wilderness advocates faced was the Forest Service itself and its industrial and motorized-recreation lobbyists. Despite a federal act in 1960, the Multiple-Use Sustained Yield Act that recognized outdoor recreation as a legitimate value of the national forests along with timber, watershed, wildlife, and other uses, the agency remained strongly oriented toward consumptive resource use, especially timber production. It was difficult for many in the agency to withdraw good timberland from production and set it aside.

In such a climate of opinion, it was not surprising that the interpretation by the Forest Service of what areas would qualify for wilderness designation created an intense debate about the preservation of areas in the East.[8] Even as early as 1968 the chief of the Forest Service was using "untrampled" to mean "untrammeled" as a justification for excluding lands that had signs of previous use and development.[9] The agency adopted the narrow view that only pristine, untouched wilderness areas qualified and that any history of use by humans would disqualify them for consideration. This came to be known as the "purity standards" view.

Conservationists, who believed that the Wilderness Act did not preclude areas with a history of human use, ran head-on into the Forest Service's rules. When the agency initiated a systematic review of roadless areas within the national forests, as called for in the Wilderness Act, it adhered to its purity standards and disqualified almost all land for wilderness designation in the East, including that in Wild River Valley. To head off a growing movement by conservationists to preserve eastern wilderness areas that were not pristine, the Forest Service encouraged support of a bill called the National Forests Wild Areas Act of 1972, which also reflected the purity standards. Fortunately, the bill died when Congress adjourned without acting on it. The next year, those who had come to love Wild River Valley, who had embraced the values of wilderness preservation for the valley, got their chance.

PART III

FIRE IN THE HEART

Seven

WILDERNESS VISION

The time was May 7, 1973, seventy years after the devastating fire of 1903. The event: a federal hearing in Concord, New Hampshire, to take testimony on bills to add eastern land in the White Mountain National Forest to the National Wilderness Preservation System. A delegation representing the Sierra Club in the Northeast recommended two areas be designated as wilderness—Caribou–Speckled Mountain on the Maine side in Batchelder's Grant and Wild River on the New Hampshire side in Bean's Purchase. Other conservation organizations also spoke in favor, including the Appalachian Mountain Club, The Nature Conservancy, and the Natural Resources Council of Maine.[1] But Congress had deaf ears: when the Eastern Wilderness Areas Act was signed into law by President Gerald Ford on January 3, 1975, an act which added fifteen national wilderness areas in the East to the Wilderness Preservation System and designated seventeen more for further study, no areas in Wild River Valley were among them (see Appendix B).

About this time, in the mid-1970s, citizens brought enough pressure to bear on Congress that the body directed the Forest Service to initiate another inventory of roadless areas. The main valley of Wild River, which had been the subject of much public interest, was one area studied and it received "one of the highest ratings for wilderness attributes in the eastern United States."[2] Appeals were also made to include the Caribou–Speckled Mountain area in the study, but they were not successful.

The middle of the 1970s also saw the Forest Service under mounting pressure to manage the forest for multiple use. Increasing numbers of citizens valued the national forests for more than just timber production. As a result, laws were enacted to address management concerns, including one that required the Forest Service to initiate the first ten-year plan for the White Mountain National Forest.[3] During the planning process

Summit of Caribou Mountain looking west into Wild River Valley
PHOTOGRAPH BY DEAN B. BENNETT

in the early 1980s, attempts were made to include both New Hampshire's Bean's Purchase and Maine's Caribou–Speckled Mountain areas in federal bills, but again these efforts failed. With support for a Wild River area wilderness bill languishing, the Maine congressional delegation decided to instruct the Forest Service to conduct a study, and the delegation set up an ad hoc committee to advise it on the issue of establishing a Caribou–Speckled Mountain wilderness area in the ten-year plan. The committee, which represented conservationists, the timber industry, and other interests, was co-chaired by Jerry Bley of the Natural Resources Council of Maine and Burm Garland of a local wood products company.

The first break for conservationists came in the spring of 1984: the Forest Service studied the Caribou–Speckled Mountain area and determined that it contained 16,000 acres of roadless public land within the Evans Notch Ranger District.[4] The agency also sought management direction from the public through the mass mailing of a questionnaire.[5]

Summit of Caribou Mountain looking south
PHOTOGRAPH BY DEAN B. BENNETT

Over 550 people and groups responded. More than 75 percent favored wilderness, and most of those supported an option of 16,000 acres being recommended to Congress for wilderness.[6]

As a result of the committee's work and the Forest Service's study, the draft of the ten-year plan for the White Mountain National Forest recommended only 12,000 acres for a Caribou–Speckled Mountain wilderness area, withdrawing 4,000 acres of timberland in a compromise. During the winter of 1984–85, the ad hoc committee met several times to review and discuss the recommendation, and both the committee and the Forest Service continued to receive arguments for and against wilderness designation.

The strongest arguments against wilderness designation came from the timber interests and the wood products industry with support of the Sportsman's Alliance of Maine. They argued that wilderness designation would reduce the available timber supply; harm the economy of local communities; lead to an unhealthy, ugly forest; limit public recreation;

*Jerry Bley, 1985. In the mid-1980s, Jerry Bley of the Natural Resources
Council of Maine, co-chaired an ad hoc committee to advise Maine's
congressional delegation on the issue of establishing a
Caribou–Speckled Mountain wilderness area.*
PHOTOGRAPH COURTESY OF THE NATURAL RESOURCES COUNCIL OF MAINE

result in loss to the federal treasury; conflict with the more preferable
multiple-use management goal; cause loss of taxes to surrounding communities; provide more wilderness when it was not needed; and reflect
the views of a vocal minority of preservation extremists.[7]

Proponents of wilderness designation replied that studies by the
Forest Service and the Maine Department of Conservation found that
the amount of timber lost would be insignificant, the amount of wood
harvested from the National Forest would not diminish, and the quality

of logs would actually increase.[8] Wilderness, they argued, adds diversity to recreational uses. It is an important part of multiple use, which doesn't mean that every use will or should occur on the same parcel of land. For example, open-pit mining and timber harvesting on the same piece of land are incompatible, and similarly so is motorized recreational use incompatible with a wilderness experience in which one seeks peace, quiet, and solitude. They identified many uses—hunting, fishing, trapping, camping, and hiking—that are compatible with wilderness designation. They pointed out that more wilderness is needed, not less. The Caribou–Speckled Mountain area, they said, is the last area in Maine eligible for federal wilderness designation because of limited federal land in the state.[9]

After much discussion of the pro and con arguments, the ad hoc committee voted nine to two in favor of the 12,000-acre compromise, and communicated a favorable recommendation for wilderness designation to the congressional delegation and to the Forest Service. In the winter of 1985–86, the Forest Service released its final management plan for the White Mountain National Forest. As expected, the plan included a recommendation to create the 12,000-acre Caribou–Speckled Mountain Wilderness Area. However, Wild River Valley on the New Hampshire side was bypassed for wilderness recommendation, and most of it was, in effect, relegated to a holding pattern for consideration in the next planning process.

With the Forest Service's plan in place, the conservationists concentrated on obtaining congressional approval for wilderness designation. Nothing happened! For nearly three years, through the remainder of 1987, 1988, and 1989, opposition continued, especially from timber and wood products interests who kept up a strong effort against preservation. In this climate no congressional action occurred. Frustrated, the Natural Resources Council of Maine published in its January 1990 bulletin a call for Maine's congressional delegation to move forward on the Caribou–Speckled Mountain designation.[10]

The council's message apparently was heard, for on March 4, 1990, the *Maine Sunday Telegram*, a statewide newspaper, ran a headline for an editorial that read " 'New' Wilderness." The editorial went on to say:

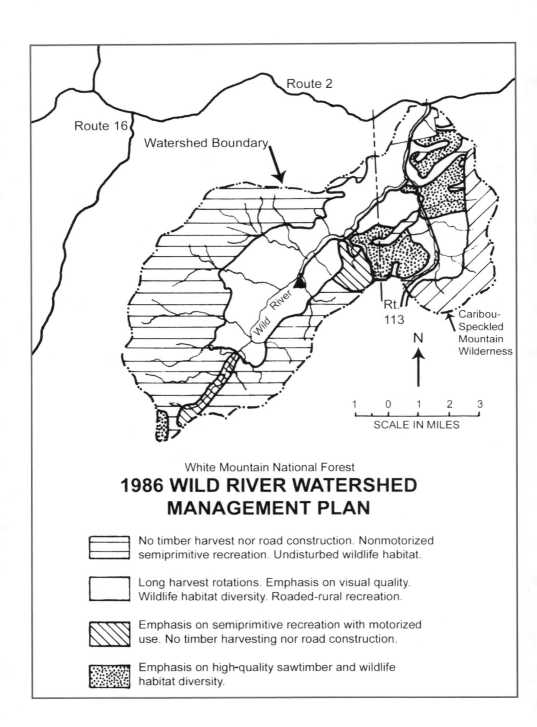

Route 2

Route 16

Watershed Boundary

Wild River

Rt.
113

N

Caribou-
Speckled
Mountain
Wilderness

1   0   1   2   3
SCALE IN MILES

White Mountain National Forest
1986 WILD RIVER WATERSHED MANAGEMENT PLAN

No timber harvest nor road construction. Nonmotorized semiprimitive recreation. Undisturbed wildlife habitat.

Long harvest rotations. Emphasis on visual quality. Wildlife habitat diversity. Roaded-rural recreation.

Emphasis on semiprimitive recreation with motorized use. No timber harvesting nor road construction.

Emphasis on high-quality sawtimber and wildlife habitat diversity.

Maine's congressional delegation announced it is filing bills to protect a large area of the White Mountain National Forest in western Maine as a wilderness preserve. . . . Action by Congress represents a final step in a plan that has been two decades in the making to extend wilderness protection to 12,000 acres in the Caribou Mountain and Speckled Mountain area. It is an unspoiled region marked by sheer cliffs, waterfalls, giant birches and breathtaking mountain scenes. . . . The Caribou–Speckled Mountain project should prove as calming as it is exhilarating.[11]

A month later, on April 18, 1990, Jerry Bley testified before the Subcommittee on Conservation and Forestry of the United States Senate Committee on Agriculture, Nutrition, and Forestry at a hearing to establish the Caribou–Speckled Mountain Wilderness. In his concluding remarks, Bley quoted a 1957 statement by Governor Percival Baxter, who singlehandedly created New England's largest wilderness, Baxter State Park—more than 200,000 acres, a great part of which would remain "forever wild":

You can't improve upon nature. That's the beauty of the park. It's natural. Baxter Park was created for a special purpose. Someday— maybe in your day—there won't be any real wild areas left. This park may be the only place where future generations can see Maine as it really was.[12]

Left: 1986 Wild River Watershed Management Plan. After the 1986 White Mountain National Forest planning process, a portion of Wild River Valley in the Evans Brook watershed was designated as wilderness. However, no wilderness was recommended in the main valley of Wild River on the New Hampshire side. Instead, the management plan called for roughly half of the valley to be open to timber harvesting and the remainder managed for semiprimitive recreation with no timber harvesting. Redrawn from "Management Area Map, Land and Resource Management Plan," White Mountain National Forest, New Hampshire–Maine, U.S.D.A., Forest Service, Eastern Region.

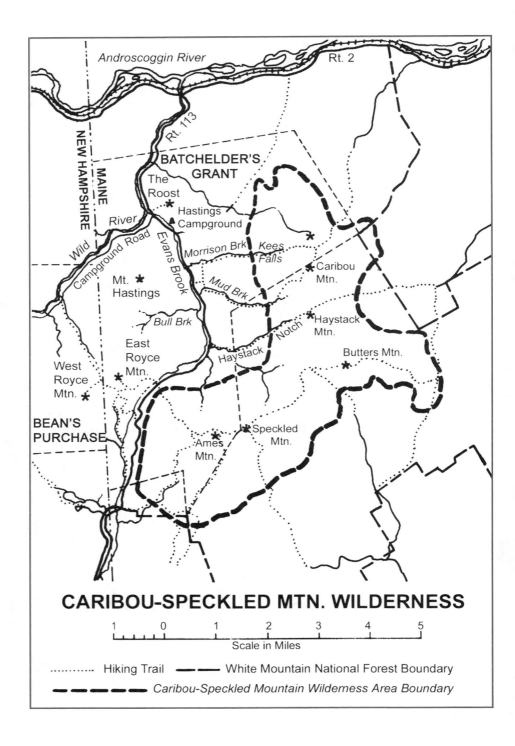

Androscoggin River

Rt. 2

Rt. 113

NEW HAMPSHIRE

MAINE

BATCHELDER'S
GRANT

The
Roost

Wild

River

Campground Road

Hastings
Campground

Morrison Brk

Kees
Falls

Evans Brook

Mud Brk

Caribou
Mtn.

Mt.
Hastings

Bull Brk

Haystack
Mtn.

East
Royce
Mtn.

Haystack

Notch

Butters Mtn.

West
Royce
Mtn.

BEAN'S
PURCHASE

Ames
Mtn.

Speckled
Mtn.

CARIBOU-SPECKLED MTN. WILDERNESS

1   0   1   2   3   4   5

Scale in Miles

.... Hiking Trail   ━━ ━━ White Mountain National Forest Boundary

━ ━ ━ ━ ━ *Caribou-Speckled Mountain Wilderness Area Boundary*

Jerry Bley, 2006. In the fall of 2006, Jerry Bley returned to the Caribou–Speckled Mountain Wilderness Area. Here, he's seen in conversation with a forester of the U.S. Forest Service.
PHOTOGRAPH BY CHARLES LEVESQUE, COURTESY OF JERRY BLEY

Left: Caribou–Speckled Mountain Wilderness Area. After an effort that lasted nearly two decades, the 12,000-acre Caribou–Speckled Mountain area in the Evans Brook part of Wild River Valley was designated a federal wilderness area.

On September 28, 1990, the bill received the signature of President George H. W. Bush, becoming Public Law No. 101-401.

Three years later the forest supervisor of the White Mountain National Forest signed the new management plan and implementation schedule for the Caribou–Speckled Mountain Wilderness. That same year the University of Maine published two separate visitor studies that found, among other things, that visitors to the new wilderness were motivated to make a trip to the area because they wanted to experience tranquility, peace, and calm, and get away from crowds and the regular routine—a testament to the remarkable renewal of nature that had taken place.[13]

So by the mid-1990s visitors to part of the Batchelder's Grant side of Wild River Valley could take comfort in knowing that it was finally returning to a semblance of the wilderness it was when the Hastings family began to assume ownership in the mid-1800s. It had taken two decades of struggle for conservationists to achieve less than half of their wilderness vision for Wild River Valley. But it would be only a few years before they would have another chance.

Eight

Bold Idea

It would have been unthinkable to the residents and businessmen of Hastings in 1899, but what was being proposed a century later by Dan Yetter and the Friends of Wild River was, in the minds of many, sensible and achievable, though admittedly ambitious. They proposed designating as wilderness the valley of Wild River and land surrounding its watershed from Route 113 on the Maine side to points along Route 16 to the west and along Route 2 to the north—more than 70,000 acres!

As a federal wilderness area, it would be "a place to find yourself," the members of the volunteer group declared in their published brochure. "In contrast to the nearby Presidential Range, Wild River offers the chance for real solitude with its circular shape and large size . . . surrounded on three sides by mountains. These mountains encompass a 27,000-acre lowland interior valley that offers a wealth of rare forest habitats for a wide range of wildlife and plants." It is "a lush valley steeped in national Heritage . . . [where] Wild River has shaped the course of the valley's history, back to a time when New England's forests were cleared for lumber." Here, they proclaimed, "is Our Future. It is rare in New England to find a place such as Wild River—where a vast, stunningly alive, intact watershed can be protected from fragmentation and development for all Americans, for all time."[1]

The Friends thought big, and they attempted to reach a big audience. The more they worked on their proposal, the more they saw it as a benefit not only to the White Mountain National Forest but to the entire New England region. In keeping with concepts of conservation biology and landscape ecology, they envisioned a Wild River wilderness area that would be a "linked chain of large wildlands" extending across the White Mountain National Forest—an opportunity for wildlife to migrate from one area to another unimpeded except by roadways. Thus, they argued,

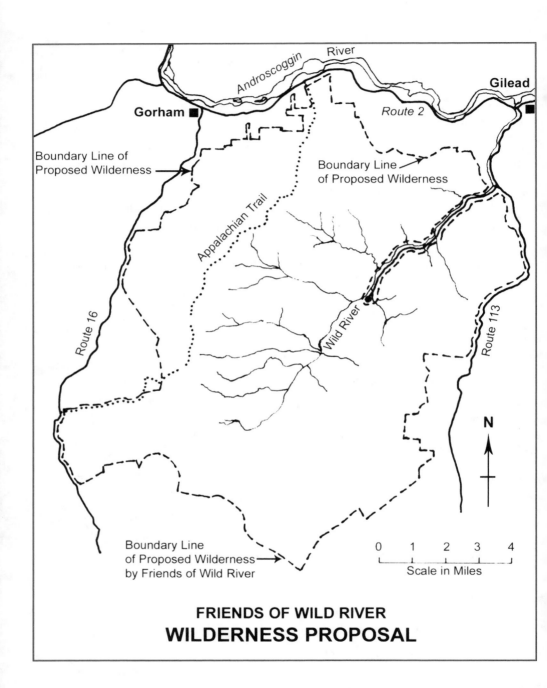

Boundary Line of
Proposed Wilderness →

Boundary Line
of Proposed Wilderness

Androscoggin   River

Gorham ■

Gilead ■

Route 2

Appalachian Trail

Route 16

Wild River

Route 113

N

Boundary Line
of Proposed Wilderness →
by Friends of Wild River

0   1   2   3   4
Scale in Miles

FRIENDS OF WILD RIVER
WILDERNESS PROPOSAL

the boundaries of a Wild River wilderness should not only include the river's complete watershed but should be moved out to the surrounding roads. To do less would result in the loss of several significant values.[2]

They contended that, by including the whole drainage of the river, their proposal would protect ecologically valuable low-elevation land. At lower elevations, winds are generally reduced in velocity, temperatures are higher, soils are deeper, and the ground is more level. Thus plant growth is more abundant and animals find more favorable habitats. They noted that the 1986 Forest Plan disproportionately preserved land located at high elevations. No land was allocated as wilderness below 800 feet in elevation.[3]

In a final argument for protecting the ecological integrity of the valley, the Friends asserted that the precolonial landscape was covered by extensive forest. Wildlife species with a preferred habitat of mature, old-growth stands of trees were able to migrate across the landscape encountering only occasional disturbed and early successional areas. Preserving the entire valley as wilderness would allow it to come closer to the presettlement landscape it once was with unhindered natural processes.[4]

The Friends did not have to start from scratch. They had the benefit of lessons learned in the two-decade-long effort that had resulted in the preservation of the Caribou–Speckled Mountain Wilderness Area. The Friends learned from that difficult struggle that they would need to have patience, do their homework, gain public support, and be willing to compromise. But even then, they knew it would not be easy, and it wasn't.

Left: Friends of Wild River Wilderness Proposal. The Friends of Wild River worked for nearly a decade in an effort to try to preserve more than 70,000 acres, including the entire valley on the New Hampshire side. The proposal would extend wilderness designation to Route 113 in Maine and beyond the valley's watershed to northern, western, and southern outer slopes. Redrawn from Friends of Wild River, Wild River: Keep It Wild, *a brochure.*

Dan Yetter's Wild River destiny had begun in 1985 when an interest in hiking led him to join the Appalachian Mountain Club (AMC). For the next decade, he hiked and backpacked in the White Mountains and on the Appalachian Trail between the mountains of New Hampshire and Katahdin in Maine. It was in Maine's expansive, ruggedly mountainous wildlands that he discovered "what a pleasure it was to spend days and nights in a remote forest."[5]

Sometime during those hiking years in the White Mountains, Yetter discovered Wild River Valley, and he fell in love with the place. A summer overnight backpacking expedition into Evans Notch and a winter cross-country ski trip on the north side of Wild River introduced him to the remote yet accessible wildness of the valley. He also spent several weekends with his New Hampshire friend and backpacking companion Tom Merrick and Tom's brother, Ed, camping just south of the valley on the other side of its mountain divide at AMC's Cold River Camp. The two brothers shared Yetter's passion for the area's remoteness, primitive trails, and mountain vistas.

Then in January 1998 something happened that set Yetter on a course that would change his life for the next decade and Wild River Valley forever. Two months earlier, in November 1997, he had met Julie Wormser of The Wilderness Society at a Northern Forest Conference in Vermont. In January she contacted Yetter to see if he would be interested in becoming a member of one of the "friends" groups she was organizing for the White Mountains' roadless areas. It was a time when the Forest Service was beginning to think about revising its 1986 Forest Plan. The timing was opportune for Yetter. As he wrote years later: "I had (1) a love for remote forests, (2) an experience of WR [Wild River] and a connection to it through the Merricks, and (3) an interest in the issue of remote forest conservation."[6] The choice was easy: he picked Wild River.

The first meeting of the Friends of Wild River was organized by Wormser in March 1998. Ross Newcomb started attending the next month and is considered by Yetter as a co-founder of the Friends. Tom

Tom Merrick (left) of the Friends of Wild River makes a point for the Friends'
wilderness proposal to Forest Service personnel. Dan Yetter is on the right.
PHOTOGRAPH BY DEAN B. BENNETT

Merrick joined shortly afterwards. In the following years, others joined, including Thomas Van Vechten, Dick Palmer, and Douglas Schwarz.[7]

That spring and summer Yetter hiked Wild River Valley's trails, taking photographs for a slide show. Newcomb also developed another slide show. While these projects would become critical elements in their campaign for public support, Yetter and Newcomb came away with something far more important: Wild River Valley had reached out and drawn them in, and in the emotional heat of its grip, they had forged a vision of wilderness for the valley that would lead to another long and difficult preservation effort. They knew from the beginning that their success would be all about numbers—the number of people who would support their efforts—and that's what they intended to get.

By March 1999 the Friends, armed with arguments and a slide show, were ready to meet with the Forest Service's planning team to discuss their view of the future of Wild River Valley as a wilderness area. And unlike the climate of resistance the Caribou–Speckled Mountain conservationists met, the Forest Service was more open to the idea. Two encouraging developments had already occurred in the Forest Service's planning process, both indicating support among citizens. Two years before, the public, in a series of meetings, had told the Forest Service that roadless areas and wilderness preservation and management were important topics to be considered in the new revision of the Forest Service's 1986 Plan.[8] And the previous year, 1998, a Forest Service supported study of New England households and Massachusetts residents had produced surprising results. The study of forest values, environmental ethics, and attitudes toward forest management showed that 94 percent of the respondents favored protecting the remaining undisturbed forests in the White Mountain National Forest, and that, overall, they rated aesthetic and ecological values of highest importance as opposed to economic values, which had received ratings of lowest importance.[9]

The Friends did not know that at the very time they were putting forth their proposal, a forester had discovered in Wild River Valley a rare old hemlock standing on a hillside, its age making it a singular figure on the landscape. If the Friends were successful in restoring the presettlement landscape, the old hemlock would be able to live out its life, perhaps another three or four hundred years, in a wilderness that would be renewed and exist in perpetuity. Once again silence would reign in its surroundings as the land repaired itself.

In February 2000 the Forest Service published its proposal for revising the Forest Plan.[10] The public's reaction revealed to the Friends the nature of the debate over the future of Wild River Valley. The range between pros and cons was extreme. One supporter of wilderness wrote:

"The Friends of Wild River's proposal should be incorporated into a Wilderness alternative also. The shape and location of the Wild River drainage is a perfect fit for congressionally designated Wilderness. . . ."[11] Another was bluntly opposed: "We don't need any more Wilderness Areas in N. H. [New Hampshire] or N. E. [New England]"[12]

Armed with citizen comments, the Forest Service continued progressing methodically and seriously through the planning process. The battle lines the Friends would face were being clearly drawn, for the Forest Plan Revision Team's revision ultimately focused on motors and recreation, timber, wilderness, and roadless areas, and wildlife. The major issues and concerns would "be addressed through alternatives in an Environmental Impact Statement."[13]

During this critical time of planning, the Friends of Wild River had been meeting monthly. Members had been giving slide shows in public locations, collecting signatures, campaigning for letters and postcards to be sent to the Forest Service and elected governmental officials, participating in public planning meetings, and giving guided hikes in Wild River to decision makers and interested citizens. One such hike occurred on September 24 in the fall of 2002. The Friends had invited the new Forest Service supervisor of the White Mountain National Forest, Thomas Wagner, and members of his staff with the purpose of making the case that Wild River should be designated as wilderness.

When people began to arrive at the Wild River parking lot on that sunny, crisp September morning, the trunk of Dan Yetter's car was open. Hanging down from a string hooked over the raised trunk lid was a colorful cloth banner depicting Noah's ark, and over it were the words "Wild River." The banner spoke not only to the need to protect the wild things in the valley for what, today, we commonly call biodiversity, but it spoke to the spiritual need for wilderness. As the day progressed, it became clear that, for many, Wild River offered a sanctuary for the human spirit—a special place to discover and nurture feelings about themselves, their relationships with others, and their connection with and responsibility to the rest of nature. And it was also obvious, considering the long distances people had driven that morning, that this special place was within easy reach of urban areas in the East.

Dan Yetter stands by a display in the Wild River parking lot prior to an informational hike with the Friends and Forest Service personnel to promote Wild River Valley as wilderness.
PHOTOGRAPH BY DEAN B. BENNETT

In the parking lot where the group gathered, there was little to suggest that it was once a place where hundreds of people carried on their lives in a village called Hastings. An early morning mist swirled up from the river a short distance away, shrouding what had been the main street in a ghostly veil—where a century earlier in the darkness of early morning, six days a week, people had trudged by the boardinghouse, past the store and post office and the school, crossed the railroad tracks, and walked by the freight barn to the sawmill from which they returned twelve hours later fatigued to a degree rarely known to most workers today. Undoubtedly the smell of freshly sawed and stacked hardwood had filled the air, and the constant whine of saws and planers and the chugging of locomotives had drowned out the sound of the river's rapids nearby.

After introductions and an orientation, the group moved from the parking lot to the river and then drove up the Wild River Campground road for a walking discussion on the Burnt Mill Brook Trail. The day was filled with frank, open, courteous give-and-take on personal reflections and professional observations about the effects of wilderness preservation on habitat preservation, visitor use, timber harvesting, roads and motorized recreation, and other management issues. When it was over, Supervisor Wagner gave some closing thoughts, saying that he was keeping an open mind. "In the end," he said, "we are all friends of Wild River."[14]

At the end of March 2003 the Forest Service released its draft of four alternatives for the plan revision process. Alternative 1 recommended no wilderness for Wild River Valley. Alternatives 2, 3, and 4 each included a wilderness area in Wild River Valley, but all the areas would be significantly smaller than what the Friends had proposed.[15] The question now was which alternative would the Forest Service recommend? The future of the old hemlock rested for the moment on that decision, for it would only be protected within the wilderness boundaries of alternatives 2 and 3.

The next year, 2004, the Forest Service released its recommendation for wilderness in Wild River Valley: it was alternative 2. Yetter, in his report on the October meeting of the Friends, wrote:

The Forest Service draft plan proposed a "preferred alternative" [alternative 2]. . . . This preferred alternative recommends to Congress that a new Wilderness be created in the upper elevation portion of the Wild River Valley. While the Forest Service's proposal considers a much smaller area than the Friends of Wild River recommended [about a third of the 70,000 acres the Friends sought, or

23,700 acres], this is still a very positive step which we feel greatly improves the likelihood that a Wild River Wilderness will be created in the next few years.[16]

On November 18, 2005, the Forest Service issued a press release stating:

> Forest Supervisor Tom Wagner announced that the White Mountain National Forest has issued a revised Forest Plan for the management of national forest land in New Hampshire and Maine. Wagner said, "The Final Revised Plan and Final Environmental Impact Statement are being released today. I believe . . . Alternative 2 reflects a balanced management approach for the White Mountain National Forest."[17]

The decision had been made; the recommendation for Wild River wilderness was now official. Through the next spring and summer of 2006, all seemed to be moving smoothly. No appeals against the recommendations of the Forest Plan were made. The Friends of Wild River and the Friends of Sandwich Range, which also had a wilderness area approved in the plan, joined forces to urge the support of the New Hampshire congressional delegation. The delegation introduced legislation which was subsequently combined into a bill that would also add wilderness in the Green Mountain National Forest in Vermont. That bill was named the New England Wilderness Act. The act passed the United States Senate unanimously.

Then, trouble! An Associated Press article published in the *Conway Daily Sun* on September 22 announced that Governor Douglas of Vermont wrote to the Republican House Committee chairman saying that "unfortunately, [the bill] goes well beyond the plan, and what many

Right: Federally designated wilderness in Wild River Valley—2006. On December 1, 2006, President George W. Bush signed the New England Wilderness Act of 2006, the final step in the designation of approximately 23,700 acres of wilderness in Wild River Valley. Redrawn from the map and area proposed on February 6, 2006, and approved by Congress and the president of the United States.

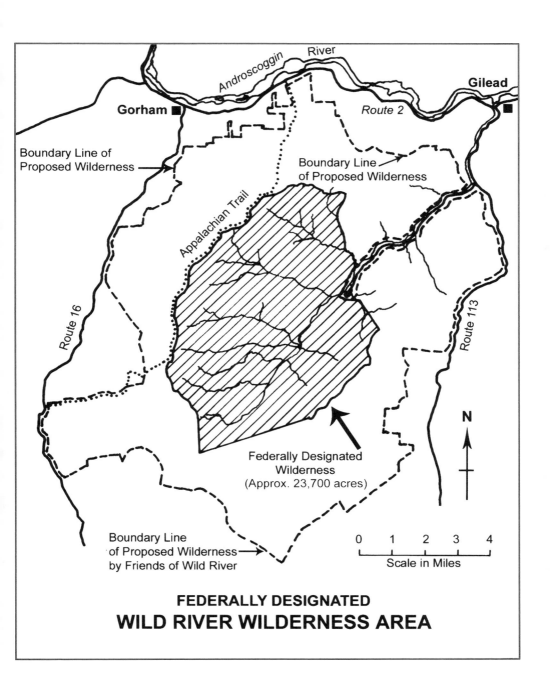

Boundary Line of
Proposed Wilderness

Boundary Line
of Proposed Wilderness

Androscoggin River

Gorham ■

Gilead ■

Route 2

Appalachian Trail

Route 16

Route 113

Federally Designated
Wilderness
(Approx. 23,700 acres)

N

Boundary Line
of Proposed Wilderness
by Friends of Wild River

0 1 2 3 4
Scale in Miles

FEDERALLY DESIGNATED
WILD RIVER WILDERNESS AREA

Vermonters believe is appropriate in terms of additional wilderness. . . . The bill calls for wilderness designation in towns that have been adamantly opposed to such designation."[18] He was successful in blocking the bill, for five days later, the *Concord Monitor* headlined: "House plan to guard wilderness fails."[19]

A flurry of activity ensued. On Thursday, September 28, the Associated Press announced that a compromise had been reached with Vermont's governor.[20] The next day Yetter announced word that "the revised Senate NH–VT Wilderness Bill passed the Senate."[21] It then moved to the House in hopes that it would be passed before the members left for recess.[22] It didn't happen!

Disappointment ran deep. Weeks passed. On Monday, November 13, the House of Representatives convened at 2:00 P.M., its first day back from recess. The New England Wilderness bill appeared a shoo-in, but because of a technical issue, the Speaker of the House did not bring up the bill for consideration. Two days later, following a brief debate, the bill passed. On December 1 President George W. Bush signed the bill into law. With a sigh of relief, conservationists could finally rest, assured that a significant portion of the valley was protected as a federal wilderness.

Nine

UNEXPECTED WITNESS

The old hemlock was a true survivor. It had lived through a time when men had entered its natural world, severely disrupted ecological processes, and destroyed components of ecological integrity. It had lived through the fire and floods, the cutting and building, and the removal and regrowth of the forest. Now it would be surrounded once again by wilderness. It was, in a word, a living witness—and perhaps the only one of its age in the valley.

It was probably inevitable that someone would chance upon the old tree. In addition to the increasing numbers of people who came to the valley for outdoor recreation, the number of scientists and others interested in collecting data in the field also increased. The latter part of the twentieth century had seen a growing awareness and interest in the idea of biological diversity, or, more popularly, biodiversity, as a measure of environmental health. In 1976 the National Forest Management Act required the Forest Service to "provide for diversity of plant and animal communities based on the suitability and capability of the specific land area . . . [and to manage for viable populations of] all existing native and desired non-native plants, fish, and wildlife species."[1] Over time, biodiversity came to mean (to the Forest Service) all the natural communities and species that comprise an area, the species that live in them, and the ecological processes of which species are a part and upon which they depend, such as nutrient cycling.[2]

The change in attitude toward Wild River Valley and other natural areas as a result of the interest in biodiversity is quite amazing when you juxtapose the goals of those who owned the valley in the year 1900 with the goals for the valley a century later. Today the valley's manager, the Forest Service, acknowledges that "most ecological processes in the Forest were affected by intensive harvest in the late 1800s and early

1900s."[3] The Forest Service also notes that "the loss of soil following the 1903 fire led to less productive sites, and consequently a change in species composition."[4] Now, in the present, while some processes such as wind disturbance still function naturally as they always have, others, such as the accumulation of large woody debris in streams, are still recovering, and the Forest Service's goal is to encourage continued recovery and "move hydrologic and terrestrial processes toward proper functioning conditions where feasible."[5]

In the last decades of the 1900s methods of restoring and maintaining biodiversity were developed in the ecological scientific community. This meant that an increasing amount of field survey work and literature reviews were carried out.[6] Today, because of this management direction, we know that Wild River Valley contains a broad array of habitats for wildlife, including extensive areas of hardwood, mixed wood, and softwood forest habitats. These forested areas range from large areas of mature trees to small patches of young forest and herbaceous openings. And most surprising, given the valley's history, a handful of old-growth stands have been discovered. Other habitat areas that are nonforested also exist, including exposed ledges, wetlands, brooks and streams, and the river itself. As researchers continued to explore the valley and habitats that have been allowed to return to a semblance of the natural world in which the old hemlock grew up, they discovered evidence of survivors of that world as well as species that are of concern because of threats to their viability.[7]

In the early 1990s three significant river terrace forests were discovered occupying both sides of the lower part of Wild River. The terraces are up to 1,500 feet in width and range from over 6 feet to 65 feet above the river's scour zone. Parts of low and occasionally flooded terraces are covered with sandy soils. Others with old stream channels have swampy areas on which hemlock, red maple, and black ash grow. There are terraces dominated by red spruce and hemlock, and others where northern hardwoods, including red oak, predominate. None of the forests are strictly old-growth because of prior logging, but surprisingly, some have very old trees, such as a hemlock 239 years old and a red spruce 180 years old. One terrace, in particular, described as a "wonderful spot" by a researcher, supports an attractive stand of mature old conifers, a rarity along large streams with a logging history like that of Wild River.[8]

It is therefore not surprising that Wild River Valley, despite its history of exploitation, contains features of land and water, even patches of old trees, that have somehow survived. Some rarities have been discovered and protected, and others are being carefully watched. While many of the discoveries were the result of carefully planned surveys of particular habitats, there have been others that were just plain luck, as was the case in the discovery of the old hemlock.

To those who have seen the old tree, it is truly impressive. It isn't unusually tall, but its large diameter relative to the other nearby hemlocks immediately places it in an age range by itself. Its trunk measures three and a half feet in diameter breast high, or "d.b.h." in foresters' terms. This by itself is far from an accurate indicator of age. While hemlock trees can tolerate shade and can grow in understories that are heavily shaded by dense canopies of large trees, they grow very slowly. Saplings only two to three inches in d.b.h. may be 200 years old. At that age a hemlock tree may have lived only a quarter of its life. The eastern hemlock is a long-lived tree, 800 years or more. The record is over 900 years. Trees near 400 years old and up to 40 inches in d.b.h. are more common in old-growth stands. It is difficult to know the conditions under which this tree grew during the first decades of its life.[9]

There are, however, other indicators of old age that one may observe. The crown of the tree appears small, and although the tree is rather sparsely limbed, some limbs are quite large. This has produced a reduced canopy, giving the tree something of a craggy appearance. It has a one-sided look, giving the impression of being wind-trained. The trunk, or stem, as foresters call it, leans slightly. The trunk also has branch stubs where limbs have died and broken off. Its large roots are partially exposed, and the lower part of the tree is covered with a heavy growth of mosses and lichens. Thin layers of the tree's bark have flaked off in many places. These signs all point to a tree that is very old, perhaps more than 200 to 300 years. Knowing that hemlocks can live 800 years or more, it is conceivable that this tree is more than 400 years old.[10]

It's possible that the question of age could be put to rest by coring the

This is the centuries-old hemlock tree that lived through the clear-cutting and forest fire that ravaged Wild River Valley in the late 1800s and early 1900s.

PHOTOGRAPH BY DEAN B. BENNETT

The author determines that the old hemlock measures three and a half feet in diameter. The tree is likely several centuries old.
PHOTOGRAPH BY SHEILA K. BENNETT

tree, that is, by using a tool called an increment borer to bore into the trunk of the tree and extract a small core of wood about 5mm in diameter that extends from the bark to the center of the tree. The annual rings can then be counted to obtain a close approximation of the tree's age. The rings are formed by changes in the density of cells due to seasonal growth differences—cells being larger during rapid growth of the tree and smaller during slow growth. In coring a tree, there is always the possibility that the heart of the tree is decayed and sometimes missing, which prevents a full count of the rings. Moreover, despite a paucity of evidence that points to coring causing damage to a tree, some researchers suggest

The old hemlock displays several indicators of old age. Among them are thin layers of bark that have flaked off and a heavy growth of moss that covers parts of its base. While these signs by themselves are not completely diagnostic, they are part of a total determination that a tree is very old. PHOTOGRAPH BY DEAN B. BENNETT

that there is a level of risk to the tree in the long term by creating a pathway for disease agents to spread.[11] Some may feel that perhaps the old hemlock has been through enough, so why introduce yet another risk, no matter how slight, to the tree when it isn't really necessary. Besides, not knowing its true age adds another element of mystery surrounding the old tree.

Beneath the tree, its shade has checked the growth of fir, hemlock, and red spruce seedlings. Moss-covered logs, scattered club mosses, and stands of hobble bush cover the area immediately around the tree. Several old trees have died near the hemlock, including a conk-covered white birch and a downed, rotting beech. Nearby, a smaller hemlock is riddled with sapsucker holes. A gully about 100 feet away to the northwest holds a small brook flowing rapidly down the mountain, crossing the Basin Trail below and flowing into Blue Brook. The tree is just far enough away to be hidden by vegetation from hikers on the trail. To the south of the tree, the land rises steeply beneath a cover of conifers that spread up the mountain.

The setting is beautifully natural. A nearby log beneath the tree provides a place to relax and enjoy the tree's company and quiet presence. At times when the sun backlights the hemlock, its finely needled canopy gives a gauzy appearance. When a breeze blows lightly, flickering dabs of sunlight spatter the forest floor. At other times a calming quietness settles in, and a gentle feeling seems to permeate the atmosphere. It reminds one of the quiet serenity sometimes felt in the company of elderly people who have either made their peace with the world or shut it out altogether.

Many have expressed a feeling of going back in time when they are in wild, undisturbed natural areas. The setting of an old tree can impart this, too, and one's thoughts inevitably turn to the past. What was the tree's life like? What could it tell if it could talk? Why was it able to survive, knowing the history of this valley? Its survival seems impossible, yet the old tree exists. A search of the area for signs that would indicate past logging in the vicinity of the tree reveals clues. No stumps present themselves, nor do patterns on the surface suggest old roads or skidder trails. In fact, the ground contains pits from uprooted, wind-downed trees and mounds from those long decayed, all indicators of an undisturbed forest. The ground surface is rocky and boulder-strewn, a place where hemlock trees have a reputation of thriving. It confirms the harvesting map of the area from the mid-1900s that the tree lives just inside an area characterized as covered with boulders.

Still, the railroad had come close. A map shows a spur line constructed just southwest of Blue Brook and heading in the direction of the old tree, stopping short of it. Why did the tracks stop and why didn't loggers come into the vicinity of the tree and take the timber? Joe Taylor knows something special about the railroad in this area near the old hemlock. If asked about the old railroad here, his eyes will brighten and sparkle and his dark beard will open to reveal a big grin, for he has seen

This spur track of the Wild River Railroad encountered a steep mountain slope and stopped well away from the site of the old hemlock. The steep slope, rocky terrain, and distance from the railroad were likely among the factors that accounted for the old hemlock not being cut.

PHOTOGRAPH BY DEAN B. BENNETT

something that only a few have seen: an existing section of that railroad spur line that led toward the old hemlock. Improbable as it sounds, a complete set of rails thirty to forty feet long lies spiked to ties that now rest high and exposed on a rocky streambed. The old graveled railbed, once tightly packed around the ties, has been removed over the years by the erosive effects of the brook. The ties are made of logs of various diameters, unlike the modern, milled ties of uniform dimension that are seen under railroad tracks today. The railroad builders had taken what was at hand. The rails are heavily caked with flaking rust, showing their age of over 100 years. If you surveyed the area, you would soon realize that the direction of the rails leads toward the base of a ridge near where the old hemlock stands. It appears that the abrupt rise in the land beyond the rails effectively blocked the spur from reaching the vicinity of the old tree.[12]

The luck for the old hemlock was being in the right place. The tree grew in a terrain unsuitable for the railroad to extend farther up the valley near Blue Brook, and too rocky and difficult for easy access by the logger. Its location in the valley resulted in its escape from the fire. These are probably the reasons that it was left free to continue its influence on a renewing ecosystem as nature began reclaiming the valley.

Why the great old hemlock had not been discovered earlier and at least generally known is a mystery. Perhaps it had been seen, but there is no evidence of its being mentioned. The tree is not far from the Basin Trail, albeit out of sight. The trail is well used and well advertised, appearing in numerous publications as well as on the Internet.[13] It runs between the Basin Campground off Route 113 in Evans Notch and the Wild River Campground in the valley—a distance of four and a half miles. The trail goes up over the rim of the valley, offering spectacular views from the highland.

Of course, those using the trail had objectives other than looking for an old tree. But those who desire to find the old hemlock and are successful in locating it will find a quieter, calmer, but no less fascinating experience with nature. Dominating the landscape as it does, imposing in its size and majestic in its mountainside setting, the tree produces a sense of awe and wonder at nature's beauty. Its immensity imparts a feeling of humility. This feeling is further amplified when we consider that there are elements in the natural world, like this hemlock, that are superior to us in some ways. They have evolved in ways we have not, and because of this, they may be better adapted to live where and how they do, and in some cases, such as the old hemlock, many times longer.

By its very survival, the tree evokes a deep appreciation and respect for nature. There's a little envy mixed with admiration that comes from our encounters with living things, including people we know who have survived the seemingly impossible and have the resilience to live into old age. Luck and a gift of grit is what it takes to be a survivor, and old trees are no exception. Down deep we gather a little hope from them. This is what many people like most about being in the presence of an old tree.

In a deeper sense, the old hemlock and other old trees promote a feeling of human dependence on nature. We identify with their ability to "hang in there" despite the odds, and we realize that we, too, are dependent on the natural world around us because we are vulnerable and must somehow adapt to changes beyond our control and approach nature with a healthy caution.

Beyond our physical connection to the rest of nature, we have emotional and spiritual needs. The natural world often plays an important role in our feelings of security, happiness, comfort, and even of who we are and of our feelings toward others. On a spiritual level, nature's very complexity and beauty give us pause to consider our purpose on earth and what there is beyond us. We are encouraged to think such thoughts in the presence of the old hemlock because if offers us a place of quiet contemplation. The tree symbolizes and provides a measure of the peacefulness, tranquility, gentleness, harmony, serenity, restfulness, and unhurriedness one can find in wilderness.

Being in the presence of such a grand old tree and contemplating its beauty and meaning and our relationship to it can be uplifting to the human spirit. Knowing its history and the values that it reveals can inspire one to consider a land ethic and the preservation of wilderness, and nature's inherent values of beauty, diversity, and persistence. A tree such as this is, in fact, a remnant of a wilderness that once was—a trace of nature's past integrity—and it can evoke a desire to preserve the wild.

And if its existence today is because of someone's conscious choice to leave it be, it all the more demonstrates a spirit of caring, stewardship, and responsibility to the rest of nature—all elements that must be present if we, indeed, are to survive ourselves.

Today, thanks to Dan Yetter and the Friends of Wild River, the Forest Service, and all those who supported the final plan for Wild River Valley, the old hemlock tree will be able to live out the remainder of its life undisturbed. It now stands just inside the boundary of the Wild River Wilderness Area above the Basin Trail and Blue Brook. The tree had stood through centuries of change in the valley, perhaps beginning its life before the shores of this country were invaded by a people who saw nature differently than those who met them. Now, we have in Wild River Valley a lesson in how vulnerable the land is to abuse and degradation. It will not be easy to save the planet, but at least here in this valley, we have a magnificent symbol of what this place once was and can once again become. It demonstrates that we can rekindle nature within ourselves and come to see ourselves as one with nature. It brings hope that a change in values represented here may one day spread around the world.

Epilogue

On July 5, 2007, I attended a gathering of the Friends of Wild River and other wilderness advocates at Wild River Campground to celebrate the passage of the New England Wilderness Act of 2006. We hiked along the Basin Trail to a spot where a post had been placed. There, Dan Yetter, Ross Newcomb, and Tom Van Vechten of the Friends bolted on a sign designating the boundary of Wild River Wilderness. After a brief ceremony, we hiked back to the campground. Few of us knew that up on a wooded knoll a short distance away from the sign stood the old hemlock. How many other trees in this world will be able to witness the preservation of their surroundings and be guaranteed the opportunity to live out their full lives undisturbed?

The group I accompanied that day was made up of individuals in whom trees like the old hemlock could spark a fire in the heart for a wilder nature. The tree represents the resilience and toughness of the wilderness in the valley that once was. It keeps the primeval wilderness alive. Perhaps by the time it reaches the end of a full life, thanks to efforts of the Friends of Wild River, a mature wilderness will once again surround it, alive with the glow of the wild, warmed by the cycle of life—a continuous entropy.

The future of the old hemlock was dependent on those who saw a new wilderness for the valley, who were willing to put the idea of setting limits on human behavior to restore a wild nature above the idea of allowing a freedom to treat the natural world without regard to its ecological health and longevity. They were willing to put a protective legal boundary around land areas within which a flicker of wildness could be fanned and nurtured. They had the vision and persistence to devote decades of their lives to the task of setting the valley on a course that

Left to right: Thomas Van Vechten, Daniel F. Yetter, and Ross J. Newcomb place a boundary sign in the new Wild River Wilderness in 2007, not far from the old hemlock.
PHOTOGRAPH BY DEAN B. BENNETT

would restore its wildness. They demonstrated the same toughness as that old tree, and because of their dedicated work, all of us must now respect the boundaries they helped establish. They taught us how we can renew the spirit of our connection to the land and to each other and recognize and embrace the interdependence that exists among all things so that, like the old hemlock, the generations who grow from our scattered seeds will be able to find a quality of life in their ecological niche on the planet.

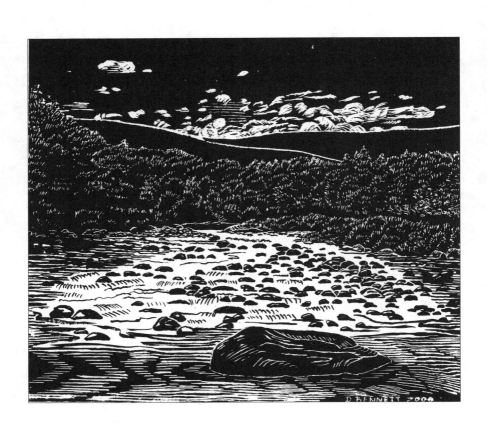

Afterword

The Glow Beyond the Valley's Rim

It is important to note that what happened in Wild River Valley is not an isolated event in wilderness preservation. Similar situations with comparable stories occurred throughout the world, including every state in the United States. A few from across this country are related below, all sharing the following commonalities: Pristine wilderness areas were exploited for economic purposes without knowledge of or regard for ecological consequences. After their natural resources were exhausted, businesses moved on. Nature began repairing and restoring itself. New values toward the natural areas emerged, leading to the formation of friends groups. Conservation-minded people, like those who worked for wilderness in Wild River Valley, had a vision that fired an imagination of what it would be like to recapture a wilderness heritage that once resided in places where it had been lost. They fanned the embers of disappearing wildland, creating a glow beyond the rim of Wild River Valley. Like the valley, many of these places had been used previously by humans, and when nature was allowed to repair and restore their damaged ecosystems, the artifacts of this use became benchmarks of changing values toward the land through time. People came to visit such areas, got to know them intimately, and discovered the secrets of their past. Some reflected on the historic values displayed by the remnants of past use and abuse of the land and its forests and came to feel an obligation of stewardship toward the land for its preservation or sustainable use.

Allegheny Plateau
If we look at efforts to preserve wilderness in America, we would discover a remarkable similarity between the story of Wild River Valley and the story of the Allegheny Plateau in northwestern Pennsylvania, some 100 miles northeast of Pittsburgh. This rugged country, drained by the

Allegheny River, was once blanketed by forests containing eastern white pine and an abundance of eastern hemlock and American beech, with lesser amounts of other hardwood species such as American chestnut, birches, and maples, and smaller populations of red oak, black cherry, and others.[1]

Like Wild River Valley, settlers arrived here in the 1700s and began harvesting the larger trees, especially the white pines. And like the Androscoggin and Wild Rivers, the Allegheny River and its tributaries were used for driving logs to mills. The arrival of the railroad era in the 1800s and the construction of logging railroads after 1880, using specially designed locomotives, also led to a period of intense commercial clear-cutting from 1890 through the first decades of the twentieth century. The plentiful hemlocks in the region provided an almost endless supply of bark for tanning. This attracted tanning companies, one of which processed 600,000 hides annually using 50,000 cords of hemlock bark. Wood alcohol mills also mushroomed for the production of methyl alcohol, acetate of lime, and charcoal. Each used thousands of cords of hardwood and drew upon coal and nearby sources of natural gas for heating.[2]

The supply of marketable wood could not be sustained. Slash fires threatened the regeneration of the forest. Under the Weeks Act of 1911, the larger lumber and chemical wood companies in 1923 began selling their holdings to the federal government, creating the Allegheny National Forest.[3] Today the national forest encompasses more than 500,000 acres. Over the years the Forest Service's management favored commercial trees such as black cherry, which is valuable for expensive veneer and furniture. A shade-tolerant tree, the black cherry constituted less than 1 percent of the trees in the presettlement forest. Today, however, it comprises up to 25 percent of the canopy trees in some stands.[4]

During the last half of the twentieth century, the passage of the Wilderness Act of 1964 and the Eastern Wilderness Areas Act of 1975 led to attempts by conservationists to seek wilderness designation for areas that had recovered from the early clear-cutting. Most of these attempts failed, except for two areas designated in 1984, totaling less than 9,000 acres, or 1.74 percent of the area's national forest.[5]

As in Wild River Valley, there are some areas in the Allegheny

National Forest that escaped the massive clear-cutting. One tract in particular, encompassing the Tionesta Scenic Area and Research Natural Area, remained uncut. The 4,100-acre parcel is dominated by huge hemlock and beech trees, some of which are nearly four feet in diameter and up to 500 years old.[6]

In 2002 the Forest Service began a planning process to revise its 1986 Forest Plan and develop a new fifteen-year management plan for the Allegheny National Forest. As did the Friends of Wild River and the earlier group of environmental organizations to preserve the Caribou–Speckled Mountain Wilderness, so did a number of groups, including the Friends of Allegheny Wilderness and its executive director, Kirk Johnson, begin a campaign to designate more wilderness in the Allegheny National Forest. They had begun laying a foundation for their effort well before the Forest Service's planning initiative. In 2003 the group released its *Citizens' Wilderness Proposal for Pennsylvania's Allegheny National Forest,* in which it identified a total of 54,460 acres in eight tracts to be protected, including the Tionesta old-growth parcel.[7]

Appealing to sentiments that acknowledge the accomplishments of local people and the attention that they can bring to a region, Kirk Johnson noted that Howard Zahniser, author of the Wilderness Act of 1964, considered his hometown to be Tionesta, located on the section of the Allegheny River that flows along the southwest boundary of the national forest. In fact, Zahniser was buried there in a cemetery plot near the river. Johnson wrote: "It is an unfortunate legacy to Howard Zahniser, a key architect of our National Wilderness Preservation System, that the land he loved as a youth has a less-than-spectacular record for wilderness designation. . . . An additional 30,000 or more acres of wilderness in the Allegheny would not only be a fitting tribute to Howard Zahniser, but would also help ensure the well-being of native Allegheny Plateau flora and fauna."[8]

Like Wild River Valley, much of the existing as well as the proposed wilderness in the Allegheny National Forest contains evidence of previous human use—remnants of farming and logging activity, including construction of the logging railroads, as well as oil and natural gas wells and other signs of resource harvesting and extraction.[9] For those who visit wilderness areas in this national forest, the evidence of human history gives visitors the advantage of seeing firsthand how human values influenced the land and how they changed as generations of people altered their perceptions of their relationship with the land. The remnants encourage visitors to contemplate the future of that relationship, even perhaps at a personal level.

The similarities between the stories do not stop here, for the Friends of Allegheny Wilderness also faced a bumpy road to preservation, reminiscent of that encountered by those working for wilderness in Wild River Valley and in the White Mountain National Forest generally. In 2002, early in the process of developing the new Forest Plan, the Forest Service's Wilderness Program manager was quoted as saying:

> The Forest Service has developed a specific protocol to inventory and evaluate proposed wilderness and applies these protocols throughout the Eastern Region on each National Forest undergoing forest plan revision. Without having detailed maps and information about the existing roads and pipe/transmission lines that seem to be throughout the proposed area, it does seem that the area in question would not meet our protocols for wilderness consideration. However, I am not saying that it will not be considered because there are mechanisms in place that allow areas outside the protocols to be considered. But at first glance and based on very limited information, it seems the Tionesta area is questionable at best.[10]

The Friends faced greater, more vocal, and direct opposition from the Allegheny Forest Alliance, an industry group that promotes "multiple use" of the national forest. Its executive director was quoted in the *Times Observer* on December 3, 2002, as saying that "there's no multiple use with wilderness." Furthermore, the reporter wrote that the spokesman for the organization "said forever designating more wilderness areas on the ANF [Allegheny National Forest] doesn't suit a region that is so economically dependent on logging the forest . . . the AFA [Allegheny Forest Alliance] would rather see existing wilderness designations ended on the ANF before seeing new areas designated. . . . 'How can anyone say wilderness is in the best interest of our successors?'"[11]

The next day, the *Times Observer* editorialized against the Allegheny Forest Alliance's position saying that it would "work to eliminate existing wilderness on the ANF. . . . That position is telling," the editorial observed and went on the say:

> What's at stake here is not the survival of the local economy or even the timber industry but access to government subsidized timber. The timber interests regard any cutback in access to federal forest land as a threat. There is good reason for that. While there is plenty of available private timberland in the Allegheny region, timber companies prefer cheap access to government subsidized stumpage on the ANF. . . . The Allegheny Forest Alliance and other industry groups like to argue that Friends of Allegheny Wilderness represents nothing but "special interests" with its plan to protect up to ten percent of the ANF with wilderness designation. What they conveniently ignore is the obvious fact that their interests are just as special.[12]

In 2007 the Forest Service published its revised Forest Plan, recommending only two new wilderness areas totaling 12,379 acres, far less than the Friends proposed. As this book goes to press, the Friends of Allegheny Wilderness continue to pursue a vigorous campaign to urge the support of its congressional delegation for the wilderness proposal in its entirety.[13]

Green Mountain National Forest

Elements of the Wild River Valley story are also seen in nearby Vermont. This state's forests, like those of New Hampshire, suffered from the effects of widespread clear-cutting in the past, but they, too, began to heal and return. In 1994 a small group of citizens, concerned about the management of Vermont's forests, especially the Green Mountain National Forest, founded Forest Watch. Through the years, the organization worked to defend wild forested areas from road building and logging, protect endangered wildlife, improve the management of public lands, and promote forestry with an ecological sensitivity.[14]

Then, in the first years of the twenty-first century, at a time when the Friends of Wild River were working for wilderness designation in Wild River Valley, Forest Watch embarked on an effort to convince the Forest Service to recommend 80,000 acres or more of wilderness in the 400,000-acre Green Mountain National Forest. By spring of 2006 the organization's efforts had resulted in a bill working its way through Congress which proposed approximately 48,200 acres of wilderness. On December 1, 40,000 acres were designated as wilderness when President George W. Bush signed the New England Wilderness Act, the same act that also included the new Wild River Wilderness Area. Still, to Forest Watch's disappointment, a number of beautiful and critical areas of potential wilderness had been left out. These would remain vulnerable to logging, road building, and various kinds of motorized recreation.[15]

There are other parallels with Wild River Valley. It's interesting to note that, like the old hemlock in Wild River Valley, an ancient oak on the shore of Lake Champlain was also seen as a witness to the changing Vermont landscape and symbolic of the past and future of the state's wilderness. Emeritus professor Carl Reidel of the University of Vermont and a past president of Forest Watch, brought attention to the old oak in the organization's newsletter. Reidel wrote that it was "already a stately tree when the French explorer Samuel de Champlain came into the lake in 1609." He noted that "history passed by this venerable tree," and today "this tree, and a few yet remaining nearby, are among the last remnants of a magnificent landscape that enraptured Champlain. . . . Here was a forest beyond our imaginations—a wilderness that would fuel a vast new commercial empire."[16]

George Washington and Jefferson National Forests

In 1969, while the passion of the environmental movement still heated the air, the Virginia Wilderness Committee formed and began identifying wilderness areas to protect in that state. By the turn of the century nearly 90,000 acres of wilderness had been designated in the state's George Washington and Jefferson National Forests, as well as another 80,000 acres of statutory wilderness in Shenandoah National Park.[17] The wilderness preservation efforts continued, and by 2006 a bill was proceeding through Congress to create seven new wilderness areas and expand six existing in Jefferson National Forest that would total more than 42,000 acres. The bill, the Virginia Ridge and Valley Act, became law when President Barack Obama signed the Omnibus Public Lands Act of 2009 on March 30, 2009.[18] At this writing, the Virginia Wilderness Committee has also recommended several wilderness areas in the George Washington National Forest to the Forest Service in the agency's current planning process, and the group has also begun a campaign with the Friends of Shenandoah Mountain to promote the designation of wilderness in the Shenandoah Mountain National Scenic Area.[19]

Like Wild River Valley, most all the lands in Virginia wilderness areas have a history of logging and marginal farming. "As such," wrote James Murray when he was president of the Virginia Wilderness Committee, "one finds physical evidence of old logging railroads, skid roads, bridges, and occasional logging equipment. Then there is also the physical and biological evidence of past farms, such as old homesites with ruined chimneys, apple trees still bearing fruit, and successional species such as Black Locust still hanging on in the second growth forest."[20]

And also like Wild River Valley, those who encounter this evidence of former human values toward nature, now preserved in place and time, cannot help but be struck with the change in our technological ability within a century or two to alter the natural environment in ways that increasingly threaten the integrity of our planet's ecological systems. If we are to deal successfully with the issues facing our planet, whether they be social or environmental, perhaps the "ultimate argument" for wilderness, as Murray suggests, is "solitude and spiritual refreshment."[21] Perspective on ourselves and our actions, as well as clarity of mind, can only help us make the best decisions for the future.

Monongahela National Forest

"A place for spiritual and emotional renewal" is also one of the important values of wilderness cited by the neighboring West Virginia Wilderness Coalition.[22] This grassroots organization is coordinated by the West Virginia Highlands Conservancy, the Sierra Club—West Virginia

Chapter, The Wilderness Society, and the Campaign for America's Wilderness. As we are beginning to see, it is evident that the Wilderness Act of 1964 spawned a widespread interest in wilderness preservation, empowering citizens in communities and regions all across America to protect wild land. The West Virginia Wilderness Coalition cites many reasons for preserving wilderness areas, and among them is renewal of the human spirit, also an important value to the Friends of Wild River.

The coalition cites "historic and cultural values" as another set of wilderness values that are "crucial to the well being of the nation."[23] West Virginia's wilderness areas contain much historic evidence of human use that gives pause for thought about our changing values toward the land and the need for a land ethic. One activist wrote that the state's "wilderness areas were almost stripped bare of timber in the late nineteenth and early twentieth centuries. The old logging days in West Virginia are viewed with the same kind of nostalgia as the old mining days. Both eastern logging and western mining were indeed mining operations—take everything economically feasible to take, and then leave. All the existing wilderness areas, with the exception of Laurel Fork, have old logging camp sites. When I discovered the Mon [Monongahela National Forest] in the late 1960s, one could still find piles of shoes for draft horses and old bottles at these sites . . . you can still find old stoves and other items too heavy to carry away."[24]

Forest fires, like those that occurred in Wild River Valley and the White Mountain National Forest, were also part of the Monongahela National Forest's history. It, too, suffered from the "disastrous logging practices of the 1880s and early 1900s in the East. Forest practices of that era laid the land bare, and devastating fires and floods followed."[25] Within the forest, the Dolly Sods Wilderness area was not only "stripped bare of all timber (except that which burned), it was also ravaged by fires started by sparks from the logging trains. Fire was not an important component of the original damp forests, but the slash and dried mosses burned readily."[26] The Monongahela National Forest, like Wild River Valley and the White Mountain National Forest, was also created under the Weeks Act of 1911, resulting from the national concern about abuse of our forests.

Four wilderness areas had been previously preserved in the 1970s and 1980s in the Monongahela National Forest, namely, Dolly Sods, Otter Creek, Cranberry, and Laurel Fork North and South. In 2006 the coalition was spearheading a campaign to convince the Forest Service to produce a new twenty-year plan that would recommend additional wilderness areas for preservation in the Monongahela. The coalition noted that the Mon "has some of the most spectacular unprotected wild places in the eastern United States. These places are threatened by a wide array of factors that could destroy their scenic beauty such as logging, mining, road building, and industrial energy development."[27]

To put the effort into perspective, the coalition also noted in 2006 that "eastern states contain only 4 percent of the National Wilderness Preservation System yet are home to nearly 60 percent of the US population. West Virginia is below average among eastern forests for amount of Wilderness acreage and number of areas. Currently, only 0.5 percent of West Virginia and less than 9 percent of the Monongahela National Forest is permanently protected as wilderness."[28] Three years later, in 2009, success came with the addition of 37,000 acres of designated wilderness in the Mon when the U.S. Congress passed the Wild Monongahela Act.[29]

Chattahoochee and Oconee National Forests
Moving into the South, Georgia ForestWatch began monitoring Chattahoochee and Oconee National Forests in 1986. The organization's mission promotes protection and restoration of "the native ecosystems of Georgia's Mountain and Piedmont public lands" and informs "citizens about the values of these landscapes."[30] Advocating for wilderness areas is part of this mission.

The last of the state's wildlands reside in its two national forests. The only old growth left from years of logging lies in the Chattahoochee. Once again we learn that the search for "solitude and spiritual renewal" is seen as a major factor that draws millions of tourists each year to wild areas.[31] Yet despite high public support for these values of wilderness, despite comments from thousands of Georgians favoring the protection of Chattahoochee's large roadless areas, and despite Georgia's inventoried roadless areas being identified as the "last best places" for experiencing remoteness and solitude, not a single one of the six largest roadless areas was put on a course for congressional designation as wilderness during the last Forest Service planning process for the Chattahoochee and Oconoee National Forests.[32] Undaunted, Georgia ForestWatch continues to actively pursue its multifaceted mission to protect the values of its unique natural features.[33]

Boundary Waters Canoe Area Wilderness

We now travel to the northern midwestern region and look at how the wilderness preservation themes of Wild River Valley are playing out in Minnesota and the Dakotas. In Minnesota, the Boundary Waters Canoe Area Wilderness (BWCAW) lies within the Superior National Forest and under the management of the United States Forest Service. In 1964 more than a million acres of this beautiful area of lakes, rivers, streams, swamps, and forests—a dream canoe country to be sure—became part of the National Wilderness Preservation System. Compromises, however, allowed logging and motorized travel.

In the mid-1970s a congressional battle erupted over logging, snow-mobiling, and motorboating that threatened the area's wilderness protection. The Friends of the Boundary Waters Wilderness formed in 1976 to fight these threats. Successful passage of a federal act in 1978 ended logging and snowmobiling and placed restrictions on the use of motorboats. Today, the BWCAW is the largest federally designated wilderness east of the Rocky Mountains and north of the Everglades. However, the need for vigilance and advocacy to protect its wilderness character has not lessened.[34]

Soon after the arrival of the twenty-first century, polls showed strong public support for wilderness protection, and the Friends conducted an "exhaustive inventory" of approximately 120,000 acres of roadless areas in the Superior National Forest. As result of this work, the Friends, in 2003, recommended wilderness protection for nearly 90,000 acres in twenty-four separate land parcels. Like Wild River Valley, many of these areas showed evidence of logging—old roads, railroad beds and bridges, an abandoned fire tower, an old mine, and other signs of past use, but the survey revealed, as one of the trained field volunteers observed, nature "healing itself."[35]

The group, in its selection of these tracts of land, noted that "contrary to popular belief, an area did not need to be totally free of the evidence of human activity to qualify for wilderness designation." Furthermore, "Aldo Leopold, a founder of the wilderness movement, affirmed this notion when he stated '. . . in any practical [wilderness] program the unit areas to be preserved must vary greatly in size and in degree of wildness.'"[36] Here in the Boundary Waters, as in Wild River Valley, visitors may find artifacts suggesting values toward wilderness.

Similarly, new values emerged in response to the return of the forest and its aura of wildness. One of those, as we have seen in Wild River Valley and elsewhere, is the value of wilderness as "a place to renew; a place to find silence, solitude, inspiration, and reflection."[37] This, too, was reflected in the visitor guide published by the Forest Service: "We often think of wilderness as a place for people. Areas to renew and refresh the soul."[38] Sigurd Olson, a famous and early advocate for wilderness and preservation of the Boundary Waters, perhaps said it best: "Some places should be preserved from development or exploitation for they satisfy human needs for solace, belonging, and perspective. In the end, we turn to nature in a frenzied, chaotic world, there to find silence, oneness, wholeness—spiritual release."[39]

Today, in 2009, the Friends group is continuing its efforts to protect as wilderness the roadless areas it recommended.[40]

Little Missouri National Grasslands

In adjacent North Dakota, at the western end of that state, lies the Little Missouri National Grasslands—one million acres of buttes and rolling plains. Here resides the heart of the Badlands Conservation Alliance, a group formed in 1999 to be "a voice for Wild North Dakota places." The members "call for ecologically functioning landscapes, protection of roadless areas, and designation of Wilderness."[41]

This is a land of plateaus rising above rippling waves of grassland, lonely buttes, and steep-sided canyons, where one can discover the sunken remains of homesteads, rock art, rings of tipis, and buffalo jumps. It was here in the 1880s that Theodore Roosevelt "developed a deep and lasting bond. That bond fostered a conservation ethic that he carried throughout his presidency."[42] That ethic is now being tested by pressures of development on the land. But it is that same ethic that drives the Badlands Conservation Alliance and Dakotans belonging to the Sierra Club and The Wilderness Society to preserve these Little Missouri grasslands.

This vast prairie country of the Dakotas, with its wild, eye-catching landforms, home of the Lakota people, was recorded by Meriwether Lewis and William Clark in 1804 on their exploration of the Missouri River to find a water route across the continent. More than two hundred years later, little of this amazing prairie that so fascinated them now remains. In 2008 the Badlands Conservation Alliance, noting an absence of grasslands in the National Wilderness Preservation System, introduced its Prairie Legacy Wilderness proposal and is working to correct this oversight.[43]

Buffalo Gap National Grasslands

Early in the first decade of the twenty-first century, the South Dakota Grasslands Wilderness Coalition, a broad group of conservationists, Native American tribes, ranchers, outdoor sportspeople, and businesses, advanced a proposal to designate as wilderness approximately 70,000 acres of the Buffalo Gap National Grasslands. This proposal built on a recommendation by the Forest Service to designate about 39,000 acres of the area as wilderness. As of early 2009, the coalition was still working to have the proposal introduced and passed by Congress.[44]

This area, like Wild River Valley, is a land with evidence of a human history. Native Americans used it for food, shelter, medicine, and burial sites. Later, fences, stock dams, dugouts, livestock structures, trails, buried pipelines, and other changes on the land by ranchers, homesteaders, and developers appeared across the landscape. With wilderness designation, some uses will continue, but some of the evidence of past use will gradually be overtaken by nature and fade into the background. It will become even more a place of nurture for the natural world and the human spirit.

In a world where we exercise so much control over the rest of nature, we must guard against becoming complacent about our need to exercise that control with compassion for other creatures and with an eye toward sustainability. However, not only do we need to see this natural world as necessary to meet our physical needs, but we need to see it as essential to serving our psychological and spiritual needs. Sigurd Olson wrote that the real function of wilderness "will always be as a spiritual backlog in the high-speed mechanical world in which we live."[45] That "wilderness gives us places to rejuvenate our spirits," is also expressed by Protect South Dakota's Wild Places Campaign as one of the ways our lives are enriched by wildlands.[46] Black Elk, the spiritual leader of the Lakota, who lived from 1863 to 1950, described the effect of the Black Hills on his own spirit:

> . . . I was standing on the highest mountain of them all and round about beneath me was the whole hoop of the world, and while I stood there I saw more than I can tell; I understood more than I saw; for I was seeing in a sacred manner the shape of all things in the spirit and the shape of all shapes as they must live together like one being."[47]

In 2006 Janet Gordon Branum, in her column for the *Brookings Register,* wrote: "Those of us who inhabit South Dakota and the hundreds of thousands more who visit each year recognize that we are blessed with magnificent places to get away from the often stressful busyness of our lives to enjoy the quiet wonder of a prairie that feels endless."[48]

Red Rock Wilderness

Going west to Utah, the Southern Utah Wilderness Alliance finds inspiration in the words of "the Dean of Western Writers" and environmentalist Wallace Stegner: "The Utah deserts and plateaus and canyons are not a country of big returns, but a country of spiritual healing, incomparable for contemplation, meditation, solitude, quiet, awe, peace of mind and body."[49] Thus, the goal of the preservation group: "To protect Utah's remaining nine million acres of wild desert lands . . . one of the world's most unique landscapes—where towering buttes, sweeping plateaus, and intimate canyons are enveloped by a rare and breathtaking silence. This is the land of the Old West and the ancient Anasazi. It is wilderness at its best. . . ."[50]

For more than two decades, the organization has worked to bring wilderness protection to these millions of acres of federal public lands, known as America's Red Rock Wilderness. The land is managed by the Bureau of Land Management (BLM). On January 6, 2006, the group achieved what was by no means a small victory when President George W. Bush signed legislation to protect 100,000 acres as wilderness, though a relatively small amount of this is in the Red Rock Wilderness. On April 2, 2009, America's Red Rock Wilderness Act to protect 9 million acres of the area as wilderness was introduced simultaneously in the House and Senate, and at this writing, the bill is currently in committees.[51] Meanwhile, the future of this land area is severely threatened by proposed oil and gas drilling and off-road vehicle abuse.

Grand Canyon

On October 31, 2002, twenty-five organizations, collectively representing approximately 5.5 million American citizens, sent a letter to the superintendent of the Grand Canyon National Park. Under the name Grand Canyon Wilderness Alliance, the organizations presented comments in response to the National Park Service's planning process for the park. Their comments were made in the context of our need for healthy ecosystems and our need for the preservation of the spiritual character of wilderness. The Alliance noted that:

> The preservation of wilderness character is the paramount directive of the Wilderness Act. By selecting the word 'character,' the authors of the Wilderness Act chose to protect more than the tangible qualities of the landscape. . . . The preservation of wilderness is, in fact, the preservation of a spiritual experience, which derives its power from the land and includes exposure to inherent risks. . . . It is through such an experience that we are allowed the opportunity to enlarge our perspective, fully open our hearts and exist with something far greater than ourselves. . . . The transpersonal encounter is rooted in

silence whether it is in a man-made structure or one carved by Nature. . . . It is the silence that allows us to attain tranquility, disengage from our normal activities, draw energy from the earth and admit a greater power to renew and sustain us. It is for this reason that wilderness is not just another type of recreational opportunity. It is profoundly unique in that it provides a deep, spiritual connection through a personal experience with the raw, primeval forces that have molded our planet.[52]

The Alliance further commented on the framework for wilderness management in the Colorado River Management Plan and its goals and objectives. Notably, it drew attention to the Grand Canyon Park's previous visitor experience objectives to guide decisions on regulating public trips in the canyon. Among them was the preservation and protection of opportunities "for visitors to experience the solitude, natural conditions, primitiveness, remoteness and inspirational value of the Grand Canyon."[53]

So what happened from the efforts of the Alliance? On November 10, 2005, a press release announced: "Park Service Plan for Colorado River Leaves Wilderness High and Dry. Solitude, Special Attributes of Wild River Abandoned in Favor of Crowd Pleasing Motorized Rides."[54] The headlines said it all: the group's efforts were to no avail. But those who know and feel the draw of wildness are not easily defeated. Following that deeply disappointing decision, legal challenges were raised and continue today through the dedicated work of organizations such as the River Runners for Wilderness, who champion wilderness designation and protection of the Colorado River and its tributaries.[55]

The lessons in Arizona are not unlike those in Wild River Valley, where it took many, many years to designate a mere 12,000 acres of the Caribou–Speckled Mountain area as wilderness against the opposition of established commercial interests. And even though public polls showed overwhelming support for wilderness preservation in both New Hampshire and Arizona, the Friends of Wild River and the Grand Canyon Wilderness Alliance both faced governmental resistance to accepting their wilderness proposals.

Nevada Wilderness

In the southeast corner of Nevada, where a small section of the Colorado River forms the state's boundary, lies the working ground for the Friends of Nevada Wilderness, a group whose efforts reflect the values seen among those concerned about the preservation of Wild River Valley. "Westerners," the Friends of Nevada Wilderness wrote, "are beginning to appreciate the relationship between wilderness and their own community health, be it quality of recreation, quality of water, or the quality of their landscape's ability to inspire wonder or stewardship."[56]

Since 1984 the Friends have worked to protect wild, primitive ecological settings and the cultural artifacts they contain by designating roadless areas in this region of southern Nevada as wilderness. Here, hidden in the area's mountains and valleys, lie artifacts of previous occupation and use of the land—ancient campsites, rock shelters, petroglyphs, milling stones, roasting pits, and remnants of tools and pottery of ancient peoples.[57] Here, too, is a more recent historic landmark: the Old Spanish Trail, or Mormon Road, that entered Nevada from the east and ran along the Virgin River, traversing the southern tip of the state.

Similar to Wild River Valley, there are living witnesses to the historic changes in Nevada's landscape. In the eastern part of the state, high up in the mountains, are the bristlecone pines. These are ancient trees, reaching ages of more than 4,000 years. Adapted to savage winds, cold temperatures, and poor growing sites, they produce distinctive shapes that seem to reflect solitude and the primordial, ravaged mountain areas where they live.[58]

The protection of these environments and others in Nevada that hold a precious natural and human history is the commitment of the Friends of Nevada Wilderness, and they have seen success. By the summer of 2009 the group had protected more than 3 million acres of Nevada wilderness, and they were in the midst of at least three major campaigns to protect wilderness-quality lands in the Humboldt–Toiyabe National Forest, the largest forest in the Lower Forty-eight, the Sheldon Refuge, and the Gold Butte Region. These lands offer the protection of special ecosystems, native plant species and wildlife, geological wonders, intriguing history, and opportunities to enjoy natural beauty, to experience unconfined recreation, and to "breathe solitude deep into your soul."[59]

California Wilderness

Moving to the West Coast, the California Wilderness Coalition has been active since 1976. Through advocacy and public education, the coalition's members work statewide to protect "natural landscapes that make California unique, providing clean air and water, a home for wildlife, and a place for recreation and spiritual renewal.[60]

Facing continuing threats against the state's remaining wildlands from commercial logging and mining, off-road vehicle abuse, and detrimental development, the coalition identified millions of acres of wildlands that are potential wilderness. Three programs support the coalition's work: securing federal wilderness designation; protecting wilderness and wilderness-quality public lands, lakes, and rivers; and protecting desert areas. A significant step forward occurred on March 30, 2009, when President Barack Obama signed legislation protecting over 700,000 acres of California lands.[61]

California is more than 2,500 miles away from Wild River Valley, yet the issues are much the same. The Friends of Wild River Valley, like the California Wilderness Coalition, continued a persistent and committed effort to save wild areas and provide oversight for those already designated. Both organizations slogged through political and bureaucratic formality and decision-making routine. And over time, they have made a difference by returning a little wildness to America.

Oregon Wilderness

To the north, the Oregon Natural Desert Association is also immersed in wilderness preservation. The organization's roots lie in a small group formed in 1987 to oppose the Bureau of Land Management's assessment of potential wilderness in eastern Oregon. Today, the association is a leader in protecting Oregon's native high-desert lands. In 2000 it worked successfully to remove adverse ecological impacts of domestic livestock grazing. During the past decade the organization worked tirelessly for wilderness designation of Oregon's Spring Basin with its "nearly ten thousand acres of rolling hills" and the state's Badlands—a 38,000-acre rough stretch of stony canyons and rock cauldrons with surprising areas of "soft airy land, green mossy rocks, and grandfather juniper standing through the centuries."[62] These efforts paid off with the signing of the Omnibus Public Lands Act of 2009 by President Barack Obama. The act permanently protects 31,000 acres of wilderness in the Badlands and 8,600 acres identified in the Spring Basin proposal.[63]

Oregon Wild is another organization that has worked since 1974 to protect and restore the state's wildlands and waters. Working with partners, legislators, and others, this group provided key support for the protection of 202,000 acres of Oregon's wilderness through the Omnibus Public Lands Act of 2009, including Mount Hood, the Columbia River Gorge, Soda Mountain, Copper Salmon, Spring Basin, and the Badlands.[64]

Alaskan Panhandle

Our final stop in this survey of wilderness areas and campaigns by friends-of-wilderness groups is the Alaskan Panhandle. Here, in a 1,000-mile stretch of coastline from Ketchikan to Kodiak, is the "largest temperate old-growth rainforest remaining in the world."[65] At the southern end is America's largest national forest, the Tongass, nearly 17 million acres covering an area the size of West Virginia. (By comparison, the White Mountain National Forest in which Wild River Valley resides is only about three-quarters of a million acres.) At the northern end lies the Chugach National Forest, America's second largest national forest at 5.5 million acres in size.

This region, by any measure, is a distinctive natural area. Average annual rainfall varies from 167 inches for Cordova in the Chugach to 74 inches in Kodiak. Sitka spruce and western hemlock grow more than 200 feet tall and live up to 1,000 years. Grizzly bears, wolves, wolverines, eagles, and wild salmon find their homes here. "The Tongass is one of the last places in North America where every plant and animal species that existed before European contact is still here."[66] The Tongass surrounds Admiralty Island, most of which is national monument and wilderness. The island is home for "one of the world's densest populations of brown bears and nesting eagles."[67]

While most of the region remains ecologically undefiled, more than a million acres have been clear-cut since the 1960s, thousands of miles of logging roads have been built, crude oil is still found on the beaches of Prince William Sound from the *Exxon Valdez* spill, and the area faces proposals for more road construction, mining, and oil development.[68] The picture that emerges is remindful of the plight of Hastings Village. In its publication, *Ghost Trees: Measuring the Vanished Forests of Southeast Alaska*, the Southeast Alaska Conservation Council writes:

Because it logged unsustainably, the [logging] industry has jeopardized the opportunity to use that wood to build a smaller, more stable industry . . . manufacturing, high value-added, finished products. . . . Now the pulp mills have closed . . . today's Southeast Alaska timber industry continues trying to log large volumes of the best remaining trees, threatening community stability. . . .[69]

It was inevitable that citizens would become concerned about the threats to the wild nature of this region and its ecological and psychological values. Those of the Alaska Rainforest Campaign wrote: "Visitors are drawn by the spectacular landscape of mountains, glaciers, and forest, by the chance to see wildlife, catch fish, and enjoy world-renowned recreational adventures. Most of all, people come to experience an awe-inspiring sense of wildness."[70] The power of this landscape on those seeking to protect it is evident in their description of it as "vast, awe-inspiring, untamed land and wildlife"[71] with "superlative wilderness characteristics such as solitude, remote recreation . . . and . . . features of scientific, educational, scenic, or historic value that make them worthy of protection."[72]

In 1970 the Southeast Alaska Conservation Council formed a coalition with other Southeast Alaskan groups to oppose timber industry plans to clear-cut 98 percent of the commercial timber of the Tongass National Forest. In the early 1990s the coalition took a leadership role in forming the Alaska Rainforest Campaign. Additionally, Admiralty Island formed a friends group dedicated to its own protection. Today, these groups and others work to protect a substantial portion of this remarkable rainforest area in an unimpaired condition while encouraging human uses compatible with this goal.[73]

* * *

As we have seen from Maine to Alaska, from the very beginnings of land preservation in Wild River Valley to the protection of the Alaskan Rainforest, volunteers proved to be the backbone of advocacy organizations' efforts to designate wilderness. These are people who represent the widespread change in values toward the land and the redefinition of our relationship with the rest of nature that occurred in the twentieth century. These are people who have experienced the effect of wild nature on the human spirit, understand the importance of safeguarding our ecosystems, and feel a responsibility for land protection.

There is one other element of commonality between the Alaskan Rainforest and Wild River Valley. It is found in the concluding section of the Southeast Alaska Conservation Council's *Ghost Trees*:

> [The Ghost Trees] remind us how magnificent the Tongass once was and hold us accountable for its future. . . . To conserve a living forest, we must protect what remains of its wild, beating heart—the special places, the roadless areas, the most magnificent remaining forest stands in all their grandeur and natural riches. Only then will we have met our historic responsibility to find a way to live in balance and harmony with this great land. . . . [74]

This is the message, too, from the old hemlock on that mountainside in Wild River Valley.

Appendix A

Timeline for Wild River Valley

500–360 mya	Major geologic events form the valley's bedrock structure and deformation patterns. (mya = millions of years ago)
40,000–13,000 B.P.	The Laurentide Ice Sheet forms in northern latitudes, grinds its way over the valley, and retreats, leaving the landscape sculpted, barren of vegetation, covered by rocks of various sizes, and softened by deposits of silt, sand, and gravel. (B.P. = before the present)
13,000 B.P.	Revegetation commences.
ca. 11,000 B.P.	Paleoindians arrive in the headwaters of the Androscoggin River and begin quarrying stone for tools on Mount Jasper. Tundra plant communities inhabit the tops of tall mountains. Valleys are becoming closed woodlands.
ca. 10,000 B.P.	Trees spread throughout the valley.
ca. 8,000–5,000 B.P	Hemlock trees come to the valley.
ca. 5,000 B.P.	A massive hemlock die-off occurs, but the species begins to return after a few hundred years.
ca. 3,000–500 B.P.	Indigenous people begin making pottery, invent the birchbark canoe, and develop agriculture.
ca. 1,500–1,000 B.P.	The hemlock population begins to decrease and take its place as a common component of plant communities in the valley.
ca. 1600	A hemlock tree seed forms that may one day grow into a large old hemlock in the valley and become a living witness to centuries of change that will occur. The seed takes root and slowly grows into a

	seedling in the shade of its parent tree, located near Wild River eight miles up in the valley from the river's mouth.
1675–76	King Philip's War marks a decline in the independent way of life for Native Americans in New England.
1741	Surveying of the Maine–New Hampshire state line begins and will bisect Wild River Valley.
1772	Reports are made of a small native village on the Androscoggin River near Bethel, Maine, some eight miles south of the mouth of Wild River.
	The Commonwealth of Massachusetts grants the Peabody Patent in the vicinity of the lower portion of Wild River Valley.
1791	Peabody Patent surveyed.
1804	Twenty families in the Peabody Patent successfully petition the Massachusetts Legislature to incorporate the town of Gilead.
1807	The Commonwealth of Massachusetts grants 28,882 acres on the Maine side of Wild River Valley to Josiah Bachelder, which is mistakenly spelled Batchelder's Grant.
1832	Alpheus Bean purchases most of the New Hampshire side of Wild River Valley, a 33,000-acre tract called Bean's Purchase.
1851	The Atlantic and St. Lawrence Railroad opens for traffic between Portland, Maine, and Gilead and will play a major role in changing the valley.
	David Robinson Hastings participates in the purchase of the "opening," a key piece of level, fertile land of about 150 to 200 acres at the confluence of Evans Brook and Wild River. A sawmill and dam are eventually built.
1870	Three brothers, David Robinson Hastings, John Decatur Hastings, and Major Gideon Alfonso

	Hastings, begin buying land in Batchelder's Grant.
1883	David R. Hastings and Major Gideon Hastings expand their business, which includes farming, logging, hemlock bark cutting, and sawing lumber. John D. Hastings drops out of the business.
1885	Leon Leonwood Bean, as a youth, begins hunting in Wild River Valley.
1890	Samuel D. Hobson and other entrepreneurs from Island Pond, Vermont, buy Bean's Purchase, form Wild River Lumber Company, build a mill on Wild River, and begin logging operations.
1891	Wild River Lumber Company begins construction of Wild River Railroad for hauling logs, and commences establishing a village at the "opening."
1892	The village in the "opening" is named Hastings, after Major Hastings, and begins to grow and take shape as the mills and railroad expand operations. Extensive clear-cutting of the valley is now underway.
1894	The village of Hastings has a schoolhouse, post office, store, boardinghouse, barn, shops, residences, sawmill, wood alcohol mill, engine house, and electricity.
1895	A large slash fire burns almost 5,000 acres around Moriah and Bull Brooks.
1898	Wild River Lumber Company is sold to Hastings Lumber Company, which is unconnected to the Hastings family.
1899	Six logging camps are operating with three hundred men working.
	A severe railroad accident kills three men near Camp No. 5 between Spruce and Red Brooks.
1901	Public efforts are underway by state forestry com-

	missions, the Appalachian Mountain Club, and the Society for the Protection of New Hampshire Forests to prevent destructive forest practices in the White Mountains.
1903	A devastating forest fire burns more than 12,000 acres in the upper part of Wild River Valley in Bean's Purchase. The old hemlock survives.
1905	The Hastings family buys out Hastings Lumber Company, including the wood alcohol mill, and forms the Hastings Chemical Company.
	Major Hastings dies at the age of eighty-four. The family carries on its business in Batchelder's Grant.
1911	The Weeks Act becomes law, creating a National Forest Reservation Commission to acquire lands in watersheds of navigable streams that are to be managed and protected by the United States Department of Agriculture through the Forest Service.
1914	Bean's Purchase is sold to the federal government.
1918	The Hastings Chemical Company sells most of Batchelder's Grant to the federal government.
1922	A New Hampshire State Game Refuge is created on Bean's Purchase.
1929	The "opening" is sold to the federal government. All of Wild River Valley is now under the management of the United States Forest Service.
1933–37	The Civilian Conservation Corps operates its Wild River Camp at the former site of Hastings Village in the "opening."
1936	The CCC finishes construction of the Evans Notch Road, now Route 113, providing easy access into Wild River Valley from two directions.
1947–52	Approximately 2,500 acres, including an area near the old hemlock, is harvested for timber. The

old hemlock survives.

1960	The federal government enacts multiple-use management in national forests in which outdoor recreation is specifically recognized as a use.
1964	The Wilderness Act for preservation of federal wilderness areas is signed into law by President Lyndon B. Johnson.
1973	A federal hearing on designation of the Caribou–Speckled Mountain area in Batchelder's Grant and Wild River Valley in Bean's Purchase is held in Concord, New Hampshire.
1974–76	Congress passes the federal legislation requiring the Forest Service to undertake comprehensive planning of its lands for a "proper balance" of use.
1983	The Maine congressional delegation establishes an ad hoc committee to advise it on the establishment of a Caribou–Speckled Mountain wilderness area.
1984	A Forest Service study determines that the Caribou–Speckled Mountain area contains 16,000 acres of roadless public land.
1985–86	The Forest Service releases its final ten-year management plan for the White Mountain National Forest with a recommendation to create a Caribou–Speckled Mountain Wilderness Area of 12,000 acres. The Wild River area in Bean's Purchase is bypassed and put into a holding pattern for future consideration as wilderness.
1990	President George H. W. Bush signs a bill creating the Caribou–Speckled Mountain Wilderness Area.
1997	The Forest Service begins preliminary work on a new fifteen-year management plan for the White Mountain National Forest.
1998	The Friends of Wild River is formed to promote the designation of Bean's Purchase on the New

Hampshire side of Wild River Valley as a federal wilderness area.

1999   The old hemlock is discovered above Blue Brook near the Basin Trail, a living witness to possibly four centuries of change in Wild River Valley.

2002   The Friends of Wild River conduct an informational hike with the Forest Service supervisor and staff members to discuss wilderness preservation of the valley.

2005   The Forest Service releases its final Forest Plan and Environmental Impact Statement recommending 23,700 acres of land for wilderness designation in Wild River Valley, including the site of the old hemlock.

2006   The New England Wilderness Act, designating recommended wilderness areas in Vermont and New Hampshire, including Wild River Valley, makes its way through Congress and is signed into law on December 1 by President George W. Bush.

2007   The Friends of Wild River place a boundary marker for the Wild River Wilderness Area on the Basin Trail near the old hemlock.

Appendix B

1975 Eastern Wilderness Area Designations

Wilderness Areas	*Wilderness Study Areas*
Sipsey Wilderness, Alabama	Belle Starr Cave Area, Arkansas
Caney Creek Wilderness, Arkansas	Dry Creek Area, Arkansas
Upper Buffalo Wilderness, Arkansas	Richland Creek Area, Arkansas
Bradwell Bay Wilderness, Florida	Sopchoppy River Area, Florida
Beaver Creek Wilderness, Kentucky	Rock River Canyon Area, Michigan
Presidential Range–Dry River Wilderness, New Hampshire	Sturgeon River Area, Michigan
Joyce Kilmer–Slickrock Wilderness, North Carolina	Craggy Mountain Area, North Carolina
Ellicott Rock Wilderness, South Carolina, North Carolina, and Georgia	Wambaw Swamp Area, South Carolina
Gee Creek Wilderness, Tennessee	Mill Creek Area, Virginia
Bristol Cliffs Wilderness, Vermont	Mountain Lake Area, Virginia
Lye Brook Wilderness, Vermont	Peters Mountain Area, Virginia
James River Face Wilderness, Virginia	Ramsey's Draft Area, Virginia
Dolly Sods Wilderness, West Virginia	Flynn Lake Area, Wisconsin
Otter Creek Wilderness, West Virginia	Round Lake Area, Wisconsin
Rainbow Lake Wilderness, Wisconsin	Cranberry Area, West Virginia
Cohutta Wilderness, Georgia and Tennessee	Big Frog Area, Tennessee
	Citico Creek Area, Tennessee

NOTES

Preface
1. Walter W. Wintturi, telephone conversation with author, May 4, 2002.

Chapter One: Magnificent Wildness
1. A number of sources were consulted for the story of the valley's bedrock formation—a story that, like all reconstructions of early geologic events, continues to be modified as new information comes to light and new theories are developed. See "Wild River at Gilead, Maine (Station 01054200)," M. A. Mast and J. T. Turk, *Environmental Characteristics and Water Quality of Hydrologic Benchmark Network Stations in the Eastern United States, 1963–95*, circular 1173-A (Washington, D.C.: United States Geological Survey, 1999) http://water.usgs.gov/pubs/circ/circ1173 /circ1173a/chapter06.htm (accessed July 31, 2006); and Philip H. Osberg, Arthur M. Hussey, II, and Gary Boone, eds., *Bedrock Geologic Map of Maine* (Augusta, Maine: Maine Department of Conservation, Maine Geological Survey, 1985).
2. Some parts of this section on the surficial geology of Wild River Valley drew on Woodrow B. Thompson, "Geologic Site of the Month—May 2003, Glacial Geology Highlights in the White Mountain National Forest—Part 2: Evans Notch Area and the Caribou–Speckled Mountain Wilderness, Western Maine" (Augusta, ME: Maine Department of Conservation, Maine Geological Survey, 2003) http://www. state.me.us/doc/nrimc/mgs/sites-2003/may03.htm (accessed December 16, 2004).
3. Information on the history of the eastern hemlock in Maine is based on pollen studies in George L. Jacobson, Jr., and Ronald B. Davis, "Temporary and Transitional: The Real Forest Primeval—the Evolution of Maine's Forests over 14,000 Years," *Habitat: Journal of the Maine Audubon Society* 5, no. 1 (January 1998): 26–29.
4. One study showed that the eastern hemlock is found on south-facing slopes three times as often as on north-facing slopes. See Wendy Fujikawa, "A Reconstruction of the Presettlement Forest in the White Mountains of New Hampshire" (bachelor's thesis, Brown University, 1997), Figure 3.
5. The description of the life history of the eastern hemlock drew on "Eastern

Hemlock," research by R. M. Godman and Kenneth Lancaster, in *Trees of Western North Carolina* (St. Paul, MN: United States Department of Agriculture, Forest Service, n.d.) http://Wildwnc.org/trees/Tsuga_canadensis.html (accessed March 15, 2003).

6. Information on the original forest types of the White Mountain region of New Hampshire comes from Alfred K. Chittenden, *Forest Conditions of Northern New Hampshire*, Bulletin No. 55 (Washington, D.C.: U.S. Department of Agriculture, Bureau of Foresty, 1905): 21; "Geology," Notebook: Miscellaneous Historical Information—WMNF, Section 6, White Mountain National History Project, p. 2; Bethel Historical Society, Inc., Bethel, Maine; and Fujikawa, "A Reconstruction of the Presettlement Forest," 15–17.

7. David R. Foster, "Species and Stand Response to Catastrophic Wind in Central New England, U.S.A.," *Journal of Ecology*, 76 (1988): 145.

8. David R. Foster and E. R. Boose, "Hurricane Disturbance Regimes in Temperate and Tropical Forest Ecosystems," in *Wind and Trees*, M. P. Coults and J. Grace, eds. (Great Britain: Cambridge Univ. Press, 1995): 313.

Chapter Two: Human Presence

1. Information on Paleoindians and their activities drew on Richard A. Boisvert, "Paleoindian Occupation of the White Mountains of New Hampshire," *Geographie Physique et Quaternane* 53, no.1 (1999): 159–74; Bruce J. Bourque, "Prehistoric Indians in Maine," in *Maine: The Pine Tree State from Prehistory to the Present*, Richard W. Judd, Edwin A. Churchill, and Joel W. Eastman, eds. (Orono, ME: University of Maine Press, 1995): 12–16; and Robson Bonnichsen, "The Coming of the Fluted-Point People," *Habitat: Journal of the Maine Audubon Society* 5, no. 1 (January 1988): 34–36.

2. For an overview of Maine's changing forests during post-glacial times, see George L. Jacobson, Jr., and Ronald B. Davis, "Temporary and Transitional: The Real Forest Primeval—The Evolution of Maine's Forests over 14,000 Years," *Habitat: Journal of the Maine Audubon Society* 5, no. 1 (January 1988): 26–29.

3. See Arthur Spiess, "Comings and Goings: Maine's Prehistoric Wildlife," *Habitat: Journal of the Maine Audubon Society* 5, no. 1 (January 1988): 30–33.

4. Jacobson, Jr., and Davis, "Temporary and Transitional," 26–29.

5. Information on Native cultural change and environmental relationships came from David Sanger, "The Original Native Mainers," *Habitat: Journal of the Maine Audubon Society* 5, no. 1 (January 1988): 37–41; and Bourque, "Prehistoric Indians in Maine," 28.

6. Dean R. Snow, "Eastern Abenaki," *The Northeast*, Bruce G. Trigger, ed., vol. 15, *The Handbook of North American Indians* (Washington, D.C.: Smithsonian Institution, 1978): 154–77, suggests that "the form Androscoggin (River) probably is

a corruption or analogical contamination with the name of Massachusetts governor Edmund Andross." Further, Snow lists a number of synonyms for Amarascoggin. Also see Gordon M. Day, "Arosagunticook and Androscoggin," in *In Search of New England's Native Past: Selected Essays by Gordon M. Day*, Michael K. Foster and William Cowan, eds. (Amherst, MA: University of Massachusetts Press, 1998): 227. Day favors the position that the Androscoggin Indians were known as Amarascoggins.

7. This report of an Indian settlement in this vicinity comes from an address by Dr. Nathaniel T. True on occasion of the Bethel Centennial in William B. Lapham, *History of Bethel, Formerly Sudbury Canada, Oxford County, Maine, 1768–1890* (Augusta, ME: Press of the Maine Farmer, 1891): 297–99. See also Chester B. Price, *Historic Indian Trails of New Hampshire* (Concord, NH: New Hampshire Archaeological Society, 1989), map.

8. See Snow, "Eastern Abenaki," 137; and Randall H. Bennett, *The White Mountains: Alps of New England* (Charleston, SC: Arcadia Publishing, 2003): 18.

9. See David L. Ghere, "The 'Disappearance' of the Abenaki in Western Maine: Political Organization and Ethnocentric Assumptions," in *After King Philip's War: Presence and Persistence in Indian New England*, Colin G. Calloway, ed. (Hanover, NH: University Press of New England, 1997): 83–84.

10. True, *History of Bethel*, 298.

11. For a review and analysis of important research and findings regarding the perspectives and values of indigenous people toward the natural environment, see Dean B. Bennett, *The Wilderness from Chamberlain Farm: A Story of Hope for the American Wild* (Washington, D.C.: Island Press, 2001): 33–40.

12. This was the conclusion of the scholar Colin G. Calloway in his overview of the fate of New England's indigenous peoples following King Philip's War (1675–1676). See Colin G. Calloway, "Introduction: Surviving the Dark Ages," in *After King Philip's War*, 1–2.

13. Ibid, 4.

14. See Ghere, "The Disappearance of the Abenakis," 82.

15. Jeremy Belknap, *The History of New-Hampshire*, vol. III (Dover, NH: O. Crosby and J. Varney, 1812): 10–12.

16. Library of Congress website, "American Memory, Samuel Langdon, An accurate map of His Majesty's Province of New Hampshire in New England & all the adjacent country northward. . . ." http://memory.loc.gov (accessed August 14, 2006).

17. Belknap, *History of New-Hampshire*, 10–12.

18. The Peabody Patent and history of Gilead is described in Howard C. Reiche, Jr., and Hugh G. Chapman, *The Smile of Providence: A History of Gilead, Maine, 1804–2004* (Falmouth, ME: The Long Point Press, 2004).

19. See General Court of the Commonwealth of Massachusetts to Josiah Batchelder,

June 22, 1816, Massachusetts Deeds, vol. 5, Townships and Reserve Lots, Land Office, 97–98.

20. Information on Alpheus Bean and Bean's Purchase comes from Bean Family Association to Eva Bean, March 16, 1967; and G. S. Wheeler to Eva Bean, March 1, 1967, Eva Bean Papers, vol. 6, Bethel Historical Society, Inc., Bethel, Maine.

21. William Mitchell Gillespie, *A Treatise on Land-Surveying: Comprising the Theory Developed from Five Elementary Principles; and the Practice*, eighth ed. (New York: D. Appleton & Company, 1873): iii.

22. A number of sources were consulted to determine the surveying instruments and methods used at the time: Gillespie, *Treatise on Land-Surveying*, 9, 14–25, 110–111, 126–29, 226–27, 372–76; Deborah Jean Warner, "True North—And Why It Mattered in Eighteenth-Century America," *Proceedings of the American Philosophical Society* 149, no. 3 (September 2005): 372–84; and "Changing Chains," *Backsights Magazine* (n.d.), published by Surveyors Historical Society and available online: http://www.surveyhistory.org/changing_chains.htm (accessed January 20, 2006).

23. Gillespie, *Treatise on Land-Surveying*, 21.

24. See Reiche, Jr., and Chapman, *Smile of Providence*, 8–10.

25. D. B. Wight, *The Wild River Wilderness* (Camden, ME: Down East Books, 1971): 41–44.

26. Bill Gove, "Rough Logging on the Wild River Railroad," *The Northern Logger and Timber Processer* 20, no. 7 (February 1972): 8.

27. Reiche, Jr., and Chapman, *Smile of Providence*, 42–43.

28. *The Mountaineer*, June 20, 1891.

29. Ibid, December 26, 1890.

30. L. C. Bateman, "There is Balm in Gilead: Mayor Wilson and Other City Fathers at Hastings' Camp—The Journal Man in their Midst," *Lewiston Journal Illustrated Magazine Section*, 21–26, December 1901 (Reprint, *Cold River Chronicle*, no. 32, December 2002).

31. Charles H. Hitchcock and J. H. Huntington, *The Geology of New Hampshire, Part I, Physical Geography* (Concord, NH: Edward A. Jenks, State Printer, 1874): 226.

32. J. H. Huntington and C. H. Hitchcock, *The Geology of New Hampshire, Part II, Stratigraphical Geology* (Concord, NH: Edward A. Jenks, State Printer, 1877): 127.

33. Information on minerals in Wild River Valley comes from G. C. Gazdick, et al., *Mines, Prospects, and Mineral Sites, Wilderness and RARE II Areas, White Mountain National Forest, New Hampshire* (Washington, D.C.: Department of the Interior, U.S. Geological Survey, 1988).

34. Robert A. Welsh, et al., *Mineral Investigation of Wild River RARE II Further Planning Area, Coos County, New Hampshire* (Washington, D.C.: Bureau of Mines,

U.S. Department of the Interior, 1982): 9–10.

35. Huntington and Hitchcock, *Geology of New Hampshire, Part II*, 128.

36. Welsh, et al., *Mineral Investigation*, 10–12.

37. Ibid., 12–14.

38. A note on the early cutting of white pine is in "White Mountain National Forest History Project," Notebook: Miscellaneous Historical Information—WMNF, Section 6, p. 1, Bethel Historical Society, Inc., Bethel Maine. The railroad, which was first named the Atlantic & St. Lawrence Railroad, came to have several names: Grand Trunk Railway in 1853, Canadian National Railroad in the 1920s, and St. Lawrence & Atlantic Railroad in 1989. http://www.answers.com/topic/st-lawrence-and-atlantic-raolroad

39. William G. Gove, "Rough Logging on the Wild River Railroad," *Down East* 17, no. 4 (November 1970): 33; and quote from Wight, *Wild River Wilderness*, 48.

40. See Reiche, Jr., and Chapman, *Smile of Providence*, 82; Gove, "Rough Logging," *Down East,* 9; and *Oxford Democrat*, November 30, 1860.

41. Barbara Honkala, comp., "Hastings Register," (unpublished; hereafter cited as Hastings Register).

42. Ralph Peabody remembered that a Robert [*sic*] Hastings had a birch mill at the "opening" before the Civil War. See "Hastings as told by Ralph Peabody," Eva Bean Papers, vol. 4, Hastings Lumber Company, box 33, Bethel Historical Society, Inc., Bethel, Maine.

43. *Bethel Courier*, August 3, 1860.

44. Ibid., December 30, 1859.

45. Honkala, Hastings Register.

46. L. C. Bateman, "A Visit to the Hastings Lumber Camps," *Lewiston Journal Magazine*, March 8, 1913.

47. Honkala, Hastings Register.

48. Bateman, "A Visit"; Honkala, Hastings Register; and Marian M. Pychowska, "Evans Notch, Royce and Baldface," *Appalachia: The Journal of the Appalachian Mountain Club*, 3 (1884): 265.

49. Hugh Chapman and Howard Reiche, *Hastings: The History of a Maine Lumbering Town that Emerged, Flourished and Vanished Within 25 Years (1892–1917)* (Gilead, ME: Gilead Historical Society, 2006).

50. Randall Spaulding, "Wild River Valley and the Region of the East Branch of the Pemigewasset," *Appalachia: The Journal of the Appalachian Mountain Club*, 3 (1884): 180.

51. The account of this trip and descriptions of the valley included here come from Pychowska, "Evans Notch, Royce and Baldface," 268–70.

52. Ibid., 265–66.

53. *Oxford Democrat*, January 16, 1883.

54. See *Industrial and Labor Statistics* (Waterville, ME: State of Maine, 1896): 72, for approximate figures for rate of use of hemlock bark by large tanneries in Maine.

55. *Non-Wood Forest Products from Conifers* (Rome, Italy: Food and Agriculture Organization of the United Nations, 1995): 8.

56. Ernest Ludlow Bogart, *Economic History of the American People* (New York: n.p., 1930): 115.

57. Statistics on Maine's tanning industry came from George Archibald Riley, "A History of Tanning in the State of Maine" (master's thesis, University of Maine, 1935).

58. Riley, "History of Tanning", 63.

59. Herbert L. Herget, "The Tannin Extraction Industry of the United States," *Journal of Forest History* (April 1983): 92.

60. Pychowska, "Evans Notch, Royce, and Baldface," 267–68.

61. The information on Leon Bean, his early history with Wild River Valley, and the invention of the famous Bean hunting boot was drawn from Leon Leonwood Bean, *My Story: The Autobiography of a Down-East Merchant* (Freeport, ME: Dingley Press, 1960): 15, 19, 41.

62. Ibid., 16.

63. "Bean Executives 'Get Back to Roots,'" *Maine Sunday Telegram*, June 16, 1985.

Chapter Three: Cutting Lifelines

1. These transactions are documented in Robert C. Rich to Eva Bean, December 21, 1966, Eva Bean Papers, vol. 4, Bethel Historical Society, Inc., Bethel, Maine.

2. See Robert C. Rich to Eva Bean, Eva Bean Papers, vol. 4, Bethel Historical Society, Inc., Bethel, Maine; and "Gilead Item," *Oxford Democrat*, July 15, 1890. Whether or not Samuel D. Hobson and Joseph Hobson were related is not known by the author.

3. See *Essex County Herald*, August 22, 1890.

4. Vermonter website, "Island Pond (Brighton), Vermont—Town History (courtesy of the Center for Rural Studies." http://www.vermonter.com/nek/islandpond.asp (accessed August 19, 2006).

5. Hamilton Child, *Gazetteer of Caledonia and Essex Counties, Vermont, 1764–1887* (Syracuse, NY: Syracuse Journal Co., Printers and Binders, 1887): 407–08; "The 1891 Grain Dealers and Shippers Gazetteer, Central Vermont Railway System," http://www.memoriallibrary.com/trans/RRGaz/CV/data.htm (accessed August 19, 2006); and *Essex County Herald*, July 31, 1891.

6. Ibid.

7. *The Mountaineer*, September 26, 1890.

8. Hugh Chapman and Howard Reiche, *Hastings: The History of a Maine Lumbering Town that Emerged, Flourished and Vanished Within 25 Years (1892–1917)* (Gilead,

ME: Gilead Historical Society, 2006): 5–6.

9. See *Oxford Democrat*, October 14, 1890; and *The Mountaineer*, October 17, October 31, November 7, December 5, and December 11, 1890.

10. *Essex County Herald*, July 31, 1891; and "Gilead Booms—She Will Get Ahead of Rumford Falls," *Oxford Democrat*, July 23, 1891.

11. *The Mountaineer*, August 28, 1891.

12. Ibid., September 25, 1891.

13. Ibid., October 30, 1891.

14. *Oxford Democrat*, October 18, 1891.

15. *Essex County Herald*, September 25, 1891; and William G. Gove, "Rough Logging on the Wild River Railroad," *Down East* 17, no. 4 (November 1970): 75.

16. Ralph Peabody information, "White Mountain National Forest History Project," Notebook: Miscellaneous Historical Information—WMNF, Section 6, p. 8, Bethel Historical Society, Inc., Bethel, Maine.

17. *The Mountaineer*, November 13, 1891.

18. Ibid., December 11, 1891.

19. Ibid.

20. Hastings Register, 59–60, 62.

21. *The Mountaineer*, February 26, 1892.

22. Ibid.

23. Ibid., June 10, 1892, and June 24, 1892.

24. Ibid., September 30, 1892.

25. *Oxford Democrat*, August 22, 1894.

26. "Hastings as told by Ralph Peabody," Eva Bean Papers, vol. 4, Hastings Lumber Co., box 33, Bethel Historical Society, Inc., Bethel, Maine.

27. "White Mountain National Forest History Project," p.3.

28. Gove, "Rough Logging," *Down East*, 64.

29. Information on Hastings Village's social life came from "Ralph Peabody," Eva Bean Papers, vol. 4; Gove, "Rough Logging," *Down East*, 64–65; *The Mountaineer*, February 20, 1895; and *The Mountaineer*, April 1905, in the *Oxford County Citizen*, February 14, 1963.

30. *Oxford Democrat*, August 22, 1894; *The Mountaineer*, January 2, 1895; and quote from *The Mountaineer*, April 1905, in the *Oxford County Citizen*, February 14, 1963.

31. Information on the alcohol mill came from Notebook: Miscellaneous Historical Information—WMNF, Section 6, p. 3; "The Wood Chemical Industry," from Thomas T. Taber, III, *Sawmills Among the Derricks*, book number 7 in the series *Logging Railroad Era of Lumbering in Pennsylvania* (n.p., 1975): 753–59; http://www.smethporthistory.org/crosby/wood.htm (accessed February 8, 2005); Richard A. Hale, e-mail message to author, February 13, 2005; and Henry K. Benson, *Chemical Utilization of Wood* (Washington, DC: United States Government Printing Office,

1932): 80–83, 85–87.

32. Bill Gove, "Rough Logging on the Wild River Railroad," *The Northern Logger and Timber Processer* 10.

33. Information on locomotives and trains of the Wild River Railroad came from Gove, "Rough Logging," *Northern Logger*, 23.

34. *The Mountaineer*, April 11, 1894.

35. Ibid., November 14, 1894.

36. See "Old Burns within the White Mountain Purchase Unit," Notebook: Miscellaneous Historical Information—WMNF, Section 5, p.1, Bethel Historical Society, Inc.; and Christine L. Goodale, "Fire in the White Mountains: An Historical Perspective," *Appalachia* 54, no. 3 (December 2003): 69.

37. *Oxford Democrat*, February 22, 1898.

38. *Maine Register*, Batchelder's Grant, 1898–1899.

39. Howard C, Reiche, Jr., and Hugh G. Chapman, *The Smile of Providence: A History of Gilead, Maine* (Falmouth, Maine: Long Point Press, 2004): 83.

40. *Bethel News*, April 19, 1899.

41. "Ralph Peabody," Eva Bean Papers, vol. 4.

42. *Records, United States Circuit Court, November 1900*, District of New Hampshire.

43. *Maine Register*, Batchelder's Grant, 1900.

44. "Ralph Peabody," Eva Bean Papers, vol. 4.

45. L. C. Bateman, "There is Balm in Gilead: Mayor Wilson and Other City Fathers at Hastings' Camp—The Journal Man in their Midst," *Lewiston Journal Illustrated Magazine Section*, 21–26 December 1901 (Reprint, *Cold River Chronicle*, no. 32, December 2002): 3.

46. Ibid.

47. Ibid.

48. Ibid.

49. See Society for the Protection of New Hampshire Forests website. http://www.spnhf.org/aboutus/our_history.asp (accessed January 31, 2006); and Judith Maddock Hudson, "Logging on the Northern Peaks, 1865–1912," *RMC Newsletter* (Winter 2005–2006): 5, Randolph Mountain Club website. http//www.randolphmountainclub.org (accessed July 29, 2006).

50. Report of the Secretary of Agriculture on the Southern Appalachian and White Mountain Watersheds, 1908, "Some Notes on White Mountain National Forest History," Notebook: Miscellaneous Historical Information—WMNF, Section 1, pp. 15–16, Bethel Historical Society, Inc., Bethel, Maine.

51. See "White Mountain National Forest History Project," Notebook: Miscellaneous Historical Information, Section 6, p. 1, Bethel Historical Society, Inc., Bethel, Maine.

52. *Bethel News*, May 20, 1903.

53. Ibid., May 27, 1903.

54. United States Department of Agriculture Bulletin, No. 55, Notebook: Miscellaneous Historical Information—WMNF, Section 1, p. 15, Bethel Historical Society, Inc., Bethel, Maine.

55. "Old Burns within the WMNF Purchase Unit," Notebook: Miscellaneous Historical Information—WMNF, Section 5, p. 1. Bethel Historical Society, Inc., Bethel, Maine.

56. *Oxford Democrat*, June 3, 1903.

57. *The Mountaineer*, June 10, 1903.

58. Several sources indicated the slash and windthrown trees left on steep slopes during the clear-cutting operations at this time: Alfred K. Chittenden, *Forest Conditions of Northern New Hampshire*, Bulletin No. 55 (Washington, D.C: U.S. Department of Agriculture, 1905): 77, in Notebook: Miscellaneous Historical Information—WMNF, Bethel Historical Society, Inc., Bethel, Maine; Report of the Forester for 1908, *Report of the Secretary of Agriculture on the Southern Appalachian and White Mountain Watersheds* (Washington, D.C: U.S. Department of Agriculture, 1908): 28, in Notebook: Miscellaneous Historical Information; and Gove, "Rough Logging," 26.

59. "Fire Years of 1903 and 1911," Notebook: Miscellaneous Historical Information—WMNF, Section 2, p. 6, Bethel Historical Society, Inc., Bethel, Maine.

60. For a description of the fire triangle and its components of fire ignition, see Leonard F. DeBano, Daniel G. Neary, and Peter F. Ffolliott, *Fire's Effects on Ecosystems* (New York: John Wiley & Sons, Inc., 1998): 20–22.

61. For a discussion of the effects of fire described here, see DeBano, Neary, and Ffolliott, *Fire's Effects*, 18, 79, 84–85, 108–09, 128–31, 143–45, 148, 167.

62. Descriptions of the effects of fire on animals drew on Jane Kapler, ed., *Wildland Fire in Ecosystems: Effects of Fire on Fauna* (Ogden, UT: U.S. Department of Agriculture, Forest Service, Rocky Mountain Research Station, 2000).

63. "White Mountain National Forest History Project," Notebook: Miscellaneous Historical Information—WMNF, Section 6, p. 3, Bethel Historical Society, Inc., Bethel, Maine.

64. Frederick R. Swan, Jr., "Post-Fire Response of Four Plant Communities in South-Central New York State," *Ecology* 51, no. 6 (1970): 1074–82; quoted in http://www.fs.fed.us/database/feis/plants/trees/tsucan/fire_effects.html (accessed February 7, 2006).

65. Alfred K. Chittenden, *Forest Conditions of Northern New Hampshire*, Map I, U.S. Department of Agriculture, Bureau or Forestry, Bulletin No. 55 (Washington, DC: Government Printing Office, 1905): 10.

66. *The Mountaineer*, June 10, 1903.

67. "White Mountain National Forest History Project," Notebook: Miscellaneous

Historical Information—WMNF, Section 6, pp. 1–2, Bethel Historical Society, Inc., Bethel, Maine.

68. "Old Burns within the WMNF Purchase Unit," Notebook: Miscellaneous Historical Information—WMNF, Section 5, p. 3, Bethel Historical Society, Inc., Bethel, Maine.

69. United States Geological Survey Report #13, Preliminary Statement on the White Mountains, by George Otis Smith, June 4, 1912, Notebook: Miscellaneous Historical Information—WMNF, Section 1, p. 16, Bethel Historical Society, Inc., Bethel, Maine.

70. "Fire Years of 1903–1911," Notebook: Miscellaneous Historical Information—WMNF, Section 2, p. 6, Bethel Historical Society, Inc., Bethel, Maine.

Chapter Four: Trauma Within

1."The Passing of Hastings," *Berlin Independent*, October 1904.

2. Hastings Register, 60; and *The Mountaineer*, April 1905 (Reprinted, "Hastings a Busy Community 60 Years Ago," *Oxford County Citizen*, February 14, 1963.

3. *The Mountaineer*, April 1905; Thomas T. Taber, III, *Sawmills Among the Derricks*, book number 7 in the series *Logging Railroad Era of Lumbering in Pennsylvania* (n.p.: n.p., 1975): 753, 755; L. C. Bateman, "A Visit to the Hastings Lumber Camps," *Lewiston Journal Magazine*, March 8, 1913.

4. *The Mountaineer*, April 1905.

5. Hastings Register" 61.

6. Austin H. Wilkins, *Ten Million Acres of Timber: The Remarkable Story of Forest Protection in the Maine Forestry District (1909–1972)* (Woolwich, ME: TBW Books, 1978): 30–31.

7. Judith Maddock Hudson, "Logging on the Northern Peaks, 1865–1912," *RMC Newsletter* (Winter 2005–06): 5, Randolph Mountain Club website. http://www.randolphmountainclub.org (accessed July 29, 2006).

8. "Report of the New Hampshire Forestry Commission," *Garden and Forest* (March 8, 1893): 109–10, Library of Congress website, Nineteenth Century Periodicals, Home Page. http://international.loc.gov (accessed August 29, 2006).

9. Hudson, "Logging on the Northern Peaks."

10. See the Society for the Protection of New Hampshire Forests website. http://www.spnhf.org/aboutus/our-history.asp (accessed January 31, 2006).

11. Alfred K. Chittenden, *Forest Conditions of Northern New Hampshire*, Bulletin No. 55 (Washington, D.C.: U.S. Department Agriculture, Bureau of Forestry, 1905): 9.

12. Ibid., 32–33.

13. Gene E. Likens and F. Herbert Bormann, "Environmental Challenges in the Twenty-First Century and Our Respect for Nature," *Blue Planet Prize 2003 Com-*

memorative Lecture (Tokyo, Japan: The Asahi Glass Foundation, 2003): 4.

14. Ibid, 2, 4–5.

15. See Hubbard Brook Ecosystem Study website. "Overview, Attributes of the Hubbard Brook Experimental Forest." http://www.hubbardbrook.org/research/overview/hbguidebook.htm (accessed January 31, 2005).

16. Ibid.

17. Robert S. Pierce, et al., "Nutrient Loss from Clearcutting in New Hampshire," National Symposium on Watersheds in Transition (Fort Collins, CO: n.p., 1972): 294.

18. Gene E. Likens and F. Herbert Bormann, "Effects of Forest Clearing on the Northern Hardwood Forest Ecosystem and Its Biogeochemistry," in Proceedings of the First International Congress of Ecology (Wageningen, Netherlands: Centre for Agricultural Publishing and Documentation, 1974): 335.

19. These details and a more complete explanation of connections between ecosystems are provided in Gene E. Likens and F. Herbert Bormann, "Linkages between Terrestrial and Aquatic Ecosystems," Bioscience 24, no. 8 (August 1974): 447.

20. These factors related to floods are clearly identified and described in James W. Hornbeck and C. Anthony Federer, "Forests and Floods," New Hampshire Forest Notes, 117 (Winter 1973–74): 18–21.

21. For this information and a discussion of the effects of clear-cutting on the organic layer of forest soils and implications for plant growth, see Pierce, et al., "Nutrient Loss from Clearcutting," 293; Merrill C. Hoyle, "Forest Soils in the White Mountains: What are Forest Soils?" New Hampshire Forest Notes, 86 (1965): 3–8; Merrill C. Hoyle, "Growth and Nutrition of Yellow Birch as Affected by the Nutrient Studies of a Podzol Soil," Tree Growth and Forest Soils (Corvallis, OR: Oregon State University Press, 1969): 221–33; and Leonard F. DeBano, Daniel G. Neary, and Peter F. Ffolliott, Fire's Effects on Ecosystems (New York: John Wiley & Sons, Inc., 1998): 105.

22. See Likens and Bormann, "Linkages," 448, 454.

23. G. E. Likens, et al., "Recovery of a Deforested Ecosystem," Science 199 (February 3, 1978): 495–96.

24. The Asahi Glass Foundation, Blue Planet Prize 2003 Commemorative Lectures (Tokyo, Japan: The Asahi Glass Foundation, 2003): 2.

25. Pierce, et al., "Nutrient Loss from Clearcutting," 294.

26. P. L. Marks and F. H. Bormann, "Revegetation Following Forest Cutting; Mechanisms for Return to Steady-State Nutrient Cycling," Science 176 (1972): 915.

27. See J. W. Hornbeck and S. J. Ursic, "Intensive Harvest and Forest Streams: Are They Compatible?" in Proceedings: Impact of Intensive Forest Harvesting on Forest Nutrient Cycling (Syracuse, NY: State University of New York, College of Environmental Science and Forestry, 1979): 249–62.

28. See Diane S. Noel, C. Wayne Martin, and C. Anthony Federer, "Effects of

Forest Clearcutting in New England on Stream Macroinvertebrates and Periphyton," *Environmental Management* 10, no. 5 (1986): 661–70.

29. Likens and Bormann, "Environmental Challenges," 8–9.

30. Ibid., 8.

31. See W. Wallace Covington, "Changes in Forest Floor Organic Matter and Nutrient Content Following Clear Cutting in Northern Hardwoods," *Ecology* 62, no. 1 (February 1981): 41–48.

32. G. E. Likens, et al., "Recovery of a Deforested Ecosystem," 495.

33. C. W. Martin and A. S. Bailey, "Twenty Years of Changes in a Northern Hardwood Forest," *Forest Ecology and Management* 123 (1999): 259.

34. For a discussion of forest floor microbial dynamics and research, see Laurie A. Taylor, Mary A. Arthur, and Ruth D. Yanai, "Forest Floor Microbial Biomass across a Northern Hardwood Successional Sequence," *Soil Biology and Biochemistry* 31 (1999): 431–39.

35. G. E. Likens, et. al, "Recovery of a Deforested Ecosystem," 495.

36. For a discussion of views against clear-cutting and promotion of sustainable forestry and natural values, see essays by Chris Maser, Alan Drengson, Herb Hammond, Reed F. Noss, Felice Page, Mitch Lansky, and others in Bill Devall, ed., *Clearcut: The Tragedy of Industrial Forestry* (San Francisco, CA: Sierra Club Books and Earth Island Press, 1993).

37. Katharine Webster, "A Business at Loggerheads," three parts, *Bangor Daily News*, April 16–17, 18, 19, 2005.

38. See F. Herbert Bormann and Gene E. Likens, "Catastrophic Disturbance and the Steady State in Northern Hardwood Forests," *American Scientist* 67 (1979): 660–69.

39. Chittenden, *Forest Conditions*, 65.

40. Ibid., 66–67.

41. DeBano, Neary, and Ffolliott, *Fire's Effects*, 73–79, 91.

42. Ibid., 108.

43. James K. Brown, "Ecological Principles, Shifting Fire Regimes and Management Considerations," in *Wildland Fire in Ecosystems: Effects of Fire on Flora*, James K. Brown and Jane Kapler Smith, eds., General Technical Report RMRS-GTR-42, vol. 2 (Ogden, UT: United States Department of Agriculture, Forest Service, Rocky Mountain Research Station, 2000): 189.

44. Aldo Leopold, "Lakes in Relation to Terrestrial Life Patterns," in *University of Wisconsin Symposium, Volume on Hydrology* (Madison, WI: University of Wisconsin, 1941): 17–22,.40.

Chapter Five: Nature's Renewal

1. See F. Herbert Bormann and Gene E. Likens, *Pattern and Process in a Forested Ecosystem: Disturbance, Development and the Steady State Based on the Hubbard Brook*

Ecosystem Study (New York: Springer-Verlag, 1979): 105, 117–19; and L. Jack Lyon, James K. Brown, Mark H. Huff, and Jane Kapler Smith, "Introduction," and Edmund S. Telfer, "Regional Variation in Fire Regimes," in *Wildland Fire in Ecosystems: Effects of Fire on Fauna*, Jane Kapler Smith, ed., General Technical Report RMRS-GTR-42, vol. 1 (Ogden, UT: United States Department of Agriculture, Forest Service, Rocky Mountain Research Station, 2000): 6–10.

2. Henry S. Graves, "Purchase of Land Under the Weeks Law in the Southern Appalachian and White Mountains," (Washington, D.C.: United States Department of Agriculture, Forest Service, 1911).

3. "White Mountain Foresters—Bethel," Eva Bean Papers, vol. 4, Bethel Historical Society, Inc., Bethel, Maine.

4. L. C. Bateman, "A Visit to Hastings Lumber Camps," *Lewiston Journal Magazine*, March 9, 1913.

5. "White Mountain National Forest History Project," Notebook: Miscellaneous Historical Information—WMNF, Section 6, p. 2, Bethel Historical Society, Inc., Bethel, Maine.

6. "White Mountain Foresters—Bethel," Eva Bean Papers, vol. 4, pp. 8–9, Bethel Historical Society, Inc., Bethel, Maine.

7. Graves, "Purchase of Land,"1.

8. Gifford Pinchot, *Breaking New Ground* (Washington, D.C.: Island Press, 1998): 27.

9. United States Forest Service, *Land and Resource Management Plan: White Mountain National Forest* (n.p.: United States Department of Agriculture, Eastern Region, 1986): II–3.

10. Ibid., II–1.

11. "Forester's Report in Response to an Application by Sullivan Chemical Co., for Sale of Cordwood in Bean's Purchase," May 29, 1916, pp. 4, 8, in Hastings Chemical Co. file, U.S. Forest Service, White Mountain National Forest, Androscoggin Ranger District, Gorham, New Hampshire.

12. Ibid., 10, 2.

13. D. B. Wight, *The Wild River Wilderness* (Camden, ME: Down East Books, 1971): 135.

14. The background on New Hampshire wildlife sanctuaries came from Liza Poinier, "Wildlife Management Areas: Get Out & Explore a Wonderful Wildlife Resource," *Wildlife Journal* (November-December 2004): 15; John W. Lanier to Lyle Wiggin, e-mail message, February 18, 1993; and Helenette Silver, *A History of New Hampshire Game and Furbearers*, Survey Report No. 6, New Hampshire Fish and Game Department (Concord, NH: Evans Printing Co., 1957): 125–31.

15. Iris W. Baird to Lyle Wiggin, January 11, 1993; and Lyle E. Wiggin to Iris W. Baird, January 24, 1993.

16. John W. Lanier to Lyle Wiggin, e-mail message, February 18, 1993.

17. See Bormann and Likens, *Pattern and Process*, 117–19.

18. See map "Hastings," May 11, 1926, file, U.S. Forest Service, White Mountain National Forest, Androscoggin Ranger District, Gorham, New Hampshire.

19. See "Stock Market Crash of 1929," Stock Market Crash! Net. http://www.stock-market-crash.net/1929.htm (accessed February 11, 2006).

20. Ibid.

21. See "The Great Depression: 1929–1942." http://www.u-s-history.com/pages/h1569.html (accessed February 11, 2006).

22. Jon A. Schlenker, Norman A. Wetherington, and Austin H. Wilkins, *In the Public Interest: The Civilian Conservation Corps in Maine* (Augusta, ME: University of Maine Press, 1988): 12.

23. See "Civilian Conservation Corps (CCC) 1933–1941." http://www.u-s-history.com/pages/h1586.html (accessed February 11, 2006).

24. Schlenker, Wetherington, and Wilkins, *In the Public Interest*, 14–22.

25. Ibid., 32–34, 66.

26. Ibid., 115; and Wight, *Wild River Wilderness*, 138–40.

27. *First CCC District: First Corps Area*, Official Annual (Cape Elizabeth, ME: United States Civilian Conservation Corps, Fort Williams, 1937): 61, 110.

28. Schlenker, Wetherington, and Wilkins, *In the Public Interest*, 66, 114.

29. Ibid., 114–16.

30. Ibid., 115–16.

31. "Timber Sale Map, Johnson Lumber Co., Inc., Present Compartment 63 [363]," July 7, 1944, files, U.S. Forest Service, White Mountain National Forest, Androscoggin Ranger District, Gorham, New Hampshire.

32. "Timber Sale Map, Wild River Sale, Three Year Unit," September 1947, files, U.S. Forest Service, White Mountain National Forest, Androscoggin Ranger District, Gorham, New Hampshire.

33. "Timber Sale Map, Nadeau 1950," files, U.S. Forest Service, White Mountain National Forest, Androscoggin Ranger District, Gorham, New Hampshire.

34. Wayne Millen to M. Alisa Mast, March 3, 1993, including "Wild River Drainage Location Map: Timber Sales from 1960 & Onward" and "Wild River Logging Summary Sheet," files, U.S. Forest Service, White Mountain National Forest, Androscoggin Ranger District, Gorham, New Hampshire.

Chapter Six: Different View

1. There have been many studies showing the reasons why people seek out wilderness and other natural areas. For example, see B. L. Driver, Roderick Nash, and Glenn Hass, "Wilderness Benefits: A State-of-Knowledge Review," in *Proceedings, National Wilderness Research Conference: Issues, State-of-Knowledge, Future Direc-*

tions (Washington, D.C.: U.S. Department of Agriculture, Forest Service, 1987): 294–319; Rachel Kaplan and Stephen Kaplan, *The Experience of Nature: A Psychological Perspective* (New York: Cambridge University Press, 1989): 1–340; Dean B. Bennett, "The Unique Contribution of Wilderness to Values of Nature," *Natural Areas Journal* 14, no. 3 (July 1994): 203–08; and for an example specifically related to Wild River Valley, see Douglas Schwarz, *Wild River Memories: How a White Mountain Valley Became My Bamily's "Holy Ground"* (Concord, NH: Plaidswede Publishing Co., 2002): 1–55.

2. Schwarz, *Wild River Memories,* 9.

3. For a further discussion of the idea that a land ethic can be positively influenced by artifacts of human use encountered in wilderness areas, see Dean B. Bennett, "Carving Wilderness Out of Civilization," in *On Wilderness: Voices from Maine*, Phyllis Austin, Dean Bennett, and Robert Kimber, eds. (Gardiner, ME: Tilbury House, Publishers, 2003): 30–36.

4. Aldo Leopold, *A Sand County Almanac* (New York: Sierra Club/Ballantine Books, 1970): 262.

5. Aldo Leopold, "The Wilderness and its Place in Forest Recreational Policy," *Journal of Forestry* 19, no. 7 (November 1921): 718.

6. The Wilderness Act of 1964, Public Law 88–577, 88th Congress, (September 3, 1964).

7. For an analysis of the term "untrammeled" and its effects on the implementation of the Wilderness Act of 1964, see Douglas W. Scott, "'Untrammeled,' 'Wilderness Character,' and the Challenges of Wilderness Preservation," *Wild Earth* 11, nos. 3 and 4 (Fall–Winter 2001–2002): 72–79.

8. The history of the politics of eastern wilderness preservation presented here drew on an informative discussion presented in James Morton Turner, "Wilderness East: Reclaiming History," *Wild Earth* 11, no.1 (Spring 2001): 19–27.

9. Scott, "'Untrammeled,'" 74.

Chapter Seven: Wilderness Vision

1. United States Senate Subcommittee on Public Lands of the Committee on Interior and Insular Affairs, *Eastern Wilderness Areas: Hearings on S. 316 and S. 938*, 93rd Congress, 1st sess., 1973.

2. *Mountain Treasures: Roadless Areas in the White Mountain National Forest* (n.p.: The Wilderness Society, The Appalachian Mountain Club, and Conservation Law Foundation, 1999): 16.

3. *Land and Resource Management Plan: White Mountain National Forest* (Washington, D.C.: U.S. Department of Agriculture, Forest Service, Eastern Region, 1986): 5.

4. "Caribou–Speckled Mountain Roadless Area and Response Form," United States

Forest Service, White Mountain National Forest Plans, 1984.

5. Ibid.

6. "Testimony of Jerry A. Bley, Resource Specialist of the Natural Resources Council of Maine, to the Maine Congressional Delegation on the Proposed Caribou–Speckled Mountain Wilderness Area," November 14, 1987, Bethel, Maine, unpublished, from the files of Jerry Bley, copy in possession of author.

7. For example, see Y. Leon Favreau to Michael B. Hathaway, December 13, 1984; and David F. Allen to Michael B. Hathaway, February 26, 1985.

8. Jerry Bley to Kathy DeCoster, February 28, 1985.

9. For example, see "Responses to Several Points Presented by Wilderness Opponents," unpublished, from the files of Jerry Bley, copy in possession of author; Jerry Bley to Kathy DeCoster; "Background Information—Issues Related to the Wilderness Proposal," unpublished, from the files of Jerry Bley, copy in possession of author; and "Testimony of Jerry A. Bley, November 14, 1987, Bethel, Maine.

10. Jerry Bley, "Perspective," *Natural Resources Council of Maine Bulletin* (January 1990): 4.

11. "New Wilderness," *Maine Sunday Telegram*, March 4, 1990.

12. Subcommittee on Conservation and Forestry of the Senate Committee on Agriculture, Nutrition, and Forestry, at a hearing on S. 2205, the Maine Wilderness Act of 1990, April 18, 1990, statement of Jerry A. Bley, Natural Resources Council of Maine.

13. See Jeffrey A. Michael, "Factors Affecting the Value of a Wilderness Visit: A Contingent Valuation Study of Caribou–Speckled Mountain Wilderness Visitors," (master's thesis, University of Maine, 1994); and M. Kristina McLean, "Caribou–Speckled Mountain Wilderness: A Study of Visitor Characteristics, Attitudes and Expectations," (master's thesis, University of Maine, 1995).

Chapter Eight: Bold Idea

1. Friends of Wild River, *Wild River: Keep It Wild* (n.p.: Friends of Wild River, 2002). Note: This refers to the latest brochure which was assembled by The Wilderness Society by Heather Dowey and Julie Wormser. The proposal itself was formed in 1998, appeared in a 1999 brochure, and took on map form in late 1999 or early 2000 with the help of David Publicover of the Appalachian Mountain Club. Personal communication from Dan Yetter to author, May 19, 2006.

2. Friends of Wild River to Forest Plan Revision Team, December 14, 2004.

3. Ibid.

4. Ibid.

5. Daniel Yetter to author, September 22, 2006.

6. Ibid.

7. Ibid.

8. *Need for Change: Notice of Intent and Description of Proposal for Revising the White Mountain National Forest Plan* (Laconia, NH: United States Department of Agriculture, Forest Service, 2000): 10, 15, 56–57.

9. Robert Manning, Jennifer Treadwell, Ben Minteer, and William Valliere, *Forest Values, Environmental Ethics, and Attitudes Toward National Forest Management* (Burlington, VT: University of Vermont, School of Natural Resources, 1998): 2–9.

10. *Need for Change.*

11. *Summary of Public Comment: Public Response to the Notice of Intent and Description of Proposal for Revising the White Mountain National Forest Plan* (Laconia, NH: United States Department of Agriculture, Forest Service, 2000): 84, 157, 160.

12. Ibid., 123–24.

13. "Working Paper—Wilderness Recommendation" (Laconia, NH: United States Department of Agriculture, Forest Service, 2002): 2–3.

14. Thomas G. Wagner to Friends of Wild River, during a meeting in Wild River Valley, September 24, 2002.

15. United States Forest Service, *White Mountain National Forest Plan Revision Meeting Draft Alternatives* (Laconia, NH: United States Department of Agriculture, Forest Service, 2003).

16. Daniel Yetter, e-mail message to Friends of Wild River, October 11, 2004.

17. United States Forest Service, White Mountain National Forest, press release, November 18, 2005.

18. Ross Sneyd, "Douglas seeks revisions to national forest wilderness plan," *Conway Daily Sun*, September 22, 2006.

19. Chelsea Conaboy, "House plan to guard wilderness fails; Bill aimed to protect White Mountain land," *Concord Monitor*, September 27, 2006.

20. Lisa Rathke, "Congressional delegation, Vermont governor reach compromise over wilderness," Associated Press, September 28, 2006.

21. Daniel Yetter, e-mail message to Friends of Wild River and Friends of the Sandwich Range, September 29, 2006.

22. Ibid.

Chapter Nine: Unexpected Witness

1. *Draft Environmental Impact Statement for Forest Plan Revision: White Mountain National Forest* (Milwaukee, WI: United States Department of Agriculture, Forest Service, Eastern Region, 2004): 3–3.

2. Ibid.

3. Ibid., 3–256.

4. Ibid., C–186.

5. Ibid., 3–256.

6. *Land and Resource Management Plan: White Mountain National Forest* (Washington, D.C.: United States Department of Agriculture, Forest Service, Eastern Region, 1986): III–3, 3–255.

7. *Draft Environmental Impact Statement*, 2004, 3–255.

8. See Brett Engstrom and Daniel D. Sperduto, "An Ecological Inventory of the White Mountain National Forest, New Hampshire," third-year interim report (Concord, NH: The New Hampshire Heritage Inventory, Department of Resources and Economic Development and The Nature Conservancy, Eastern Regional Office, 1994): 25–26; and Brett Engstrom, e-mail messages to author, April 9 and April 10, 2003.

9. "Eastern Hemlock," research by R. M. Godman and Kenneth Lancaster, in *Trees of Western North Carolina* (St. Paul, MN: United States Department of Agriculture, Forest Service, n.d.) http://Wildwnc.org/trees/Tsuga_canadensis.html (accessed March 15, 2003).

10. For a discussion of external attributes of ancient trees, see David W. Stahle, "Tree Rings and Ancient Forest History," in *Eastern Old-Growth Forests, Prospects for Rediscovery and Recovery*, Mary Byrd Davis, ed. (Washington, D.C.: Island Press, 1996): 333–34.

11. For a discussion of the level of risk to a tree from coring it, see The International Tree Ring Data Bank Forum website, "Frequently Asked Questions. http://www. civenv.animelb.edu.au/~argent/treering/treefaq.html (accessed June 4, 2006); and USGS Western Ecological Research Center website, "Publication Brief for Resource Managers, Does Coring Contribute to Tree Mortality?" http://www.werc. usgs.gov/pubbriefs/vanmantgempbmar2005.htm (accessed June 4, 2006).

12. From notes on a visit by the author with Joe Taylor to remnants of the Blue Brook railroad spur on September 17, 2002.

13. See, for example, Robert N. Buchsbaum, *Nature Hikes in the White Mountains*, 2nd ed. (Boston, MA: Appalachian Mountain Club, 2000): 302–06; Gene Daniell and Jon Burroughs, comp. and ed. *AMC White Mountain Guide*, 26th ed. (Boston, MA: Appalachian Mountain Club, 1996): 371–76; and White Mountain National Forest—Basin Trail and Basin Rim Trail, http://gorp.away.com/gorp/resources/us-_national_forest/nwtrails/hiking/basin.htm (accessed February 2, 2006).

Afterword: The Glow Beyond the Valley's Rim

1. For a description of the Allegheny Plateau and its natural character before settlement, see Gordon G. Whitney, "The History and Status of the Hemlock-Hardwood Forests of the Allegheny Plateau," *Journal of Ecology* 78 (1990): 443–45; and H. J. Lutz, "Original Forest Composition in Northwestern Pennsylvania as Indicated by Early Land Survey Notes," *Journal of Forestry* 28 (1930): 1101–03.

2. Whitney, "Forests of the Allegheny Plateau," 449–52.

3. Ibid., 449.

4. Newkirk L. Johnson, "Honoring a Wilderness Vision: A Proposal for Pennsylvania's Allegheny National Forest," *Wild Earth* (Summer 2002): 64.

5. Ibid., 64, 66.

6. Newkirk Johnson, "Allegheny Friends Call for Wilderness in Tionesta Area," *North Star: The Magazine of the North Country Trail Association* (April-June 2004): 16.

7. Newkirk L. Johnson, "Protecting the Allegheny will strengthen the area," *Centre Daily Times*, September 21, 2002; *Friends of Allegheny Wilderness: Protecting Pennsylvania's Wilderness Heritage*, brochure (n.p.: Friends of Allegheny Wilderness, n.d.); and *Friends of Allegheny Wilderness: The Official Newsletter of Friends of Allegheny Wilderness* 3, no. 3 (September 2003): 1.

8. Johnson, "Honoring a Wilderness Vision," 66–67.

9. Newkirk L. Johnson, "A Proposal for Tionesta Wilderness Designation in the Allegheny National Forest, Pennsylvania, USA," *Natural Areas Journal* 21 no. 4 (2001): 340, 343.

10. Johnson, "Allegheny Friends Call for Wilderness," 16.

11. Jon Sitler, "FAW blasts arguments against more ANF wilderness," *Times Observer*, December 3, 2002, A–1, A–3.

12. "Our Opinion: Whose special interests?" *Times Observer*, December 4, 2002, A–4.

13. *Friends of Allegheny Wilderness Newsletter* 7, no. 3 (September 2007): 1; *Friends of Allegheny Wilderness Newsletter* 9, no. 1 (March 2009): 1; and Friends of Allegheny Wilderness website. http://www.pawild.org (accessed June 20, 2009).

14. *Forest Watch*, "Who We Are." http://www.forestwatch.org/whoweare/whoweare.php (accessed June 20, 2006).

15. Dick Andrews, "Vermont Wilderness Bill Introduced," *Visions: Forest Watch Newsletter* (Spring 2006): 2–3.

16. Carl Reidel, "Wilderness: Envisioning a Living Legacy," *Visions: Forest Watch Newsletter* (Spring 2006): 5.

17. Virginia Wilderness Committee website, "About the Virginia Wilderness Committee." http://www.vawilderness.org/ (accessed June 22, 2006).

18. Ibid., "Virginia Wilderness Bill Introduced on Earth Day, 2004" and "Virginia Wilderness Committee Newsletter, June 2006." (accessed June 22, 2006); and Virginia Wilderness Committee website, "Virginia Ridge and Valley—VICTORY!" http://www.vawilderness.org (accessed June 20, 2009).

19. Virginia Wilderness Committee website, "Wilderness Recommendations for the GWNF." http://www.vawilderness.org (accessed June 20, 2009).

20. James Murray, e-mail message to author, April 21, 2003.

21. Ibid.

22. West Virginia Wilderness Coalition website, "What is wilderness?" http://www.

wvwild.org/wilderness_05.htm (accessed June 22, 2006).

23. Ibid.

24. Helen McGinnis, e-mail message to author, April 22, 2003.

25. The Wilderness Society website, "West Virginia's Wild Mountain Treasure: The Monongahela National Forest. http://www.wilderness.org/Library/Documents/ WVwildmountaintreasure.cfm (accessed June 22, 2006).

26. Helen McGinnis, e-mail message to author, April 22, 2003.

27. West Virginia Wilderness Coalition website, "Urge West Virginia's Delegation to Protect West Virginia Wilderness!" http://action.wilderness.org/campaign/ WVWild_tws (accessed June 22, 2006).

28. West Virginia Wilderness Coalition website, "What is wilderness?"

29. West Virginia Coalition website, "Congress passes historic Wild Monongahela Act." http://www.wvwild.org/pressroom_final_passage.htm (accessed June 20, 2009).

30. Georgia ForestWatch website, "Who We Are." http://www.gafw.org/who weare.html (accessed June 24, 2006).

31. Georgia ForestWatch website. http://www.gafw.org/ (accessed April 15, 2003).

32. Wayne Jenkins, "UPDATE: Our Georgia Roadless Areas: Going, Going, Gone?" *Forest News* (Spring 2006): 8–9.

33. See Georgia ForestWatch website for its current activities. http://www.gafw.org (accessed June 21, 2009).

34. See Friends of the Boundary Waters, *Preserving the Canoe Country Heritage: A Wilderness Study on Permanently Protecting Minnesota's Remaining Wild Places* (Minneapolis, MN: Friends of the Boundary Waters, 2003).

35. Ibid., 2, 9.

36. *Preserving the Canoe Country Heritage*, 11; and Aldo Leopold quote from Aldo Leopold, *A Sand County Almanac* (New York: Oxford University Press, 1989).

37. *Preserving the Canoe Country Heritage*, 9.

38. Superior National Forest, *Boundary Waters Canoe Area Wilderness: A Visitor Guide*, brochure (Washington, D.C.: U.S. Government Printing Office, 1996).

39. Sigurd F. Olson, Congressional Hearings, Ely, Minnesota, 1977; quoted in *Preserving the Canoe Country Heritage*, 5.

40. Friends of the Boundary Waters website, "Great news for roadless areas." http://www.friends-bwca.org (accessed June 21.2009).

41. See Badlands Conservation Alliance website. http://www.badlandsconservation.org (accessed July 1, 2006).

42. *North Dakota's Badlands*, brochure (n.p.: North Dakota Wilderness Coalition, n.d.).

43. Badlands Conservation Alliance website, "Wilderness." http://www.badlands conservationalliance.org (accessed June 21, 2009).

44. See South Dakota Grasslands Wilderness Coalition website. http://www.
sdgrasslandscoalition.org (accessed July 2, 2006); and "February 2009 Izaack Walton
League of America Progress Report by Paul Lepisto, Regional Conservation
Coordinator." http://www.iowaikes.net/files/February_2009_mo_report.doc (accessed June 21, 2009).

45. Quoted in *Cheyenne River Valley Wilderness Proposal* (n.p.: South Dakota
Grasslands Wilderness Coalition, 2003). See coalition website.

46. Sierra Club, *Protect South Dakota's Wild Places for Our Families, for Our Future*
(Rapid City, SD: Sierra Club, n.d.).

47. Ibid.

48. South Dakota Grasslands Wilderness Coalition website. (accessed July 2, 2006).

49. Quoted in *Southern Utah Wilderness Alliance* brochure (Salt Lake City, UT:
Southern Utah Wilderness Alliance, n.d.).

50. Ibid.

51. Southern Utah Wilderness Alliance website. http://www.suwa.org (accessed
July 3, 2006); and "America's Red Rock Wilderness Act of 2009." http://www.open
congress.org/bill/111-h1925/show (accessed June 21,2009).

52. "Colorado River Management Plan Scoping Comments" (Alpine, AZ: Grand
Canyon Wilderness Alliance, 2002): 2–3.

53. Ibid., 18.

54. Arizona Wilderness Coalition website. http://www.azwild.org (accessed July 4,
2006).

55. See River Runners for Wilderness website. http://www.rrfw.org (accessed June
22, 2009).

56. Friends of Nevada Wilderness, *Wilderness: Nevada's Hidden Treasure Worth
Preserving* (Reno, NV: Friends of Nevada Wilderness, n.d.):.3.

57. Friends of Nevada Wilderness, *Wilderness on the Horizon: Nevada's Mojave
Desert Region*, brochure (Reno, NV: Friends of Nevada Wilderness, 2001).

58. *Wilderness: Nevada's Hidden Treasure*, 13.

59. See Friends of Nevada Wilderness website. http://www.nevadawilderness.org
(accessed June 22, 2009).

60. California Wilderness Coalition website. http://www.calwild.org (accessed June
22, 2009).

61. Ibid. (Accessed June 22, 2009).

62. Oregon Natural Desert Association website. http://www.onda.org (accessed
April 15, 2003, and July 5, 2006).

63. Ibid. (accessed June 22, 2009).

64. Oregon Wild website. http://www.orwild.org (accessed July 6, 2006, and June
23, 2009).

65. Alaska Rainforest Campaign, *Alaska's Rainforest: The Future Is in Your Hands*

(Sitka, AK: Alaska Rainforest Campaign, n.d.): 2.

66. Ibid., 3.

67. Friends of Admiralty Island, *Brown Bears of Admiralty Island* (Juneau, AK: Friends of Admiralty Island, 2001): 2.

68. *Alaska's Rainforest*, 5.

69. Southeast Alaska Conservation Council, *Ghost Trees: Measuring the Vanished Forests of Southeast Alaska* (Juneau, AK: Southeast Alaska Conservation Council, n.d.): 6.

70. *Alaska's Rainforest*, 9.

71. Southeast Alaska Conservation Council membership brochure (Juneau, AK: Southeast Alaska Conservation Council, n.d.).

72. "The Tongass' Unique Wildlands," *The Raven Call* 25, no. 1 (Spring 2002): 5.

73. See, for example, the websites of Southeast Alaska Conservation Council. http://www.seac.org (accessed June 23, 2009); Alaska Chapter of the Sierra Club. http://www.alaska.sierraclub.org (accessed June 23, 2009); Alaska Coalition. http://www.alaskacoalition.org (accessed June 23, 2009); and Friends of Admiralty Island. http://www.friendsofadmiralty.org (accessed June 23, 2009).

74. *Ghost Trees*, 9.

INDEX

About the Author

Dean B. Bennett is professor emeritus at the University of Maine at Farmington. Born and raised in Maine, he received a Ph.D. in Resource Planning and Conservation from the School of Natural Resources at the University of Michigan with special emphasis in environmental education, a master's degree in science education from the University of Southern Maine, and an Honorary Doctor of Humane Letters from the University of Maine at Farmington.

He is a journeyman cabinetmaker, having completed a four-year apprenticeship at the F. O. Bailey Company in Portland, Maine, through the Maine State Apprenticeship Council, and after receiving a bachelor's degree in Industrial Arts Education at Gorham State Teachers College, he taught industrial arts in the Yarmouth, Maine, school system for several years. Much of his professional life, however, has been devoted to teaching, writing, and illustrating books in the fields of science and environmental education, natural history, and human relationships with nature. He served as the first environmental education school curriculum specialist in the Maine State Department of Education. He was among one hundred educators selected by UNESCO to participate in the first world environmental education conference in Belgrade, Yugoslavia. He received the Percival Baxter Award for Leadership in Wilderness Preservation from the Maine Chapter of the Sierra Club, the Environmental Activist Award for protection of the Allagash Wilderness Waterway from the Natural Resources Council of Maine, and the Teacher of the Year Award from Maine Audubon Society.

This is his ninth book in the nature/environment field. His other books include: *Maine's Natural Heritage: Rare Species and Unique Natural*

Features; *Allagash: Maine's Wild and Scenic River*; *The Forgotten Nature of New England: A Search for Traces of the Original Wilderness*; *The Wilderness from Chamberlain Farm: A Story of Hope for the American Wild; On Wilderness: Voices from Maine* (in collaboration with Phyllis Austin and Robert Kimber), and three children's books about nature, which he also illustrated. He enjoys playing a plectrum banjo and hiking, canoeing, and skiing with his wife, biologist Sheila K. Bennett, in the north woods of Maine.

For more information about outstanding books from
T<small>ILBURY</small> H<small>OUSE</small>, P<small>UBLISHERS</small>
please visit our website at
www.tilburyhouse.com